To
CLIO

Infinite Bless~
much lae

Kim X

WINGS
of
WISDOM

KIM DHALIWAL

BALBOA.PRESS
A DIVISION OF HAY HOUSE

Balboa Press books may be ordered through booksellers or by contacting:

Balboa Press
A Division of Hay House
1663 Liberty Drive
Bloomington, IN 47403
www.balboapress.com
844-682-1282

Because of the dynamic nature of the Internet, any web addresses or links contained in this book may have changed since publication and may no longer be valid. The views expressed in this work are solely those of the author and do not necessarily reflect the views of the publisher, and the publisher hereby disclaims any responsibility for them.

The author of this book does not dispense medical advice or prescribe the use of any technique as a form of treatment for physical, emotional, or medical problems without the advice of a physician, either directly or indirectly. The intent of the author is only to offer information of a general nature to help you in your quest for emotional and spiritual well-being. In the event you use any of the information in this book for yourself, which is your constitutional right, the author and the publisher assume no responsibility for your actions.

Any people depicted in stock imagery provided by Getty Images are models, and such images are being used for illustrative purposes only. Certain stock imagery © Getty Images.

Interior Image Credit: Sarah Holder/Kim Dhaliwal

Print information available on the last page.

ISBN: 979-8-7652-4388-6 (sc)
ISBN: 979-8-7652-4389-3 (hc)
ISBN: 979-8-7652-4387-9 (e)

Library of Congress Control Number: 2023913333

Balboa Press rev. date: 10/20/2023

Contents

Acknowledgements

My humblest and heartfelt gratitude to the Universe, God, Angels and the ethereal spiritual team, for granting me the opportunity of recognising the real soul within, and to align to what was and is already there, yet through life, conditioning and programming one forgets the reality of what evolution is. "Thank You" for the divine communication, tapped into the core of my consciousness to channel these words of wisdom!

I give my huge "Thanks" to both my beloved parents, who I miss sorely! They both were the strong backbone, the core essence of support, guidance and love. I endured the most challenging life lessons and an awakening that birthed this book.

I give my greatest "Thanks" to two beautiful precious priceless souls, my daughter and granddaughter. My anchor, my happiness, my everything and that catalyst of change for what and who I am today. The empowering strength and the greatest inspiration. I love you more than words can express, with every beat of my heart and every breath of my being "Thank you"

SOUL

I AM honouring the beautiful soul within me. I recognise the power within this physical vessel shines like a diamond, for I recognise my soul is a rare gem, I salute you for who you truly are. I salute all beautiful souls, may you all find the profound beauty of all that is, and may your heart echo the vibration of the infinite divine soul, of all that you are. May your soul blossom and flourish through this physical sheath, radiate and shine in the creation of all that you are. May each moment of your soul growth be graced in bountiful infinite blessings of love, hope, peace, good health & happiness. Embracing this 'gift of life' All is as it's meant to be, and flows exactly within divine timing. May your beautiful soul thrive in the infinite light of your human self. Fulfilling each lesson for the evolvement of thyself. I salute and honour you my beautiful soul.

So it is, and so mote it be!

Introduction

Transformation:

It is time now to let go of what was, and to transgress to what will be, all in this presence stance in the mindset of where you stand right now. It's like a coat that you have worn many…many years, so worn out, that the time has now come to adorn a new coat. This just isn't a random coat of clothing one may deem to think, it carries the weight of all those old past memories and experiences. It's that time to change it, it has become evident that the necessary growth of evolutionary processes has been recognised to continue in a more powerfully new way, an awareness and awakening of you in a different way, than the old self way. The new coat is for the future of the new self, and it will continue to grow and evolve in a newer way form to that of previously. It's not just a sudden change, but one that has been happening for a while and it's now becoming a new reality that has become persistent to resist the old patterns and ways. This is the next survival mode for the new paradigm. You have earned it, and now you're ready for the next step to make your own destiny a reality for you and all. Keep going with the flow and keep working towards your goals, your dreams and aspirations, and your future will come true for you in a new direction that will bring you closer to achieving what you're aiming for in life.

ONE

I AM, in oneness of life. I am the one being in centredness of my life, oneself is vast, and all it needs to create the mass of all you require. All within everything and everything within oneness. It starts with one step, one thought, one action to overcome any one process. I am the one in my perfect being. I am the one who is the foundation and structure of my one life. I take charge of me, myself and I. One just needs to pause and reflect, there is no separation, we are all ONE...only our role play differs, one entrance, one exit, one world, one planet earth. The destination may alter but there is only one journey....your journey. Make it a memorable one!

"I honour you, you beautiful soul"

On the morning of the 8th, of the 5th month-May at 4.44am. I channelled the message below, I paused at 5.05am and concluded on writing this piece at 05.50am, I noticed the current temperature 11'c. All numbers seem significantly poignant.

8-is a symbol of infinity, abundance, balance and inner stability and positivity

5 - indicates change is coming to boost freedom, transformation, transmutation, life changing for the better.

444-sign of wholeness, you are surrounded, supported powerfully by angelic realms and guidance. Nothing to fear.

05.05- (mirror number), is a major sign from the divine realm that you're about to embark on a journey of pure transformation.

11-spiritual awakening

"Embrace to embody what is your right, destiny is now to claim yours, where there was anticipation of what one deemed to question, now have the answers to avail of no questions. Soak nurture the power of your heart and soul to make your life better for you, and others, who may have been born without the depthless of the vast knowledge, and they will not have any doubt about your true intentions and worthiness of delivering them on their own path of salvation, and the way they have chosen their paths for themselves, to then step from within the past corridors and beyond to transcend to a state of complete obedience and transformation for their future. It is imperative to recognise, and remain true to oneself, for this is that power that embodies each collectively. Claim what is already rightfully yours, it has been well earned so long ago, on an arduous journey that was laid to be simply smooth flowing, yet became so difficult and painful due to structures, programs and conditions. Break free from those shackles, in recognition of freedom. The freedom that became entrapped of societal expectations of living. Question this, and you may still have not discovered you in the trajectory of your life. Take forth the steps to the almighty transition of transformation and trust the process from this point and beyond, allow that long pause of stagnation to wilt away, to pave the brightness of life that now becomes the norm for mankind as they transition to living today and beyond. What is falling around you, has to come downwards, just like a shell it cracks to birth what was within, this is the birth of you, and your new beginnings. Recognise your inner strength to overcome such obstacles. It is who you are that you don't recognise, more so than who you became through such things and that is why you have been so closed to your heart and soul. This precious soul habitually suppressed from living".

This book is personal, unique and grounded in depths of personal experience. My goal is to help readers connect, identify and stimulate their own awakening of their own existence, and resonate with their journey of life that is not just a path, but a trajectory and tapestry of living.

My book offers a poignant touch with an added sense of humour. My aim for my readers is to find the book uplifting, enlightening, amusing and helpful, but most of all the greatest gratification, is that it leaves them with a smile on their faces, joy in their hearts, and peace in their minds. Each and every one of us endures the darkness, the shadows and the mass of negativity. Some become stuck, some stride but fail, some just give up. The ones that get through are the ones that reflect, and find the purpose of what and who they are. I hope the readers can utilise this book as a tool to become a changed person, and to be left re assured that it is your own power of will to control circumstances, for a way forward to a new you! That you were already there a long time ago, it's time to awaken the fragments of the buried soul within to emerge, rebirth and to live. Awaken my beautiful soul to the love of who you are!

<u>My Journey</u>

It was short of plain sailing, and more of rocky road, having endured two major cathartic experiences that were the catapult to a dawning of what was to unfold and become.

Let me tell you a story; following on from my first book "Storms of life" I thought I had made an exclusive transition into the empowerment club. In my mindset the second book, which is what you are reading now, was going to be published within 2 years. Each time the goal post moved further and further, there were many reasons, which were the excuses, and truthfully there was never an excuse just me not being in control of myself. It is not what you know but what you have yet to know.

Our journey of life begins with so many lessons the good, the bad, and the ugly. As we thread along our path with all the various diversions, it's a reverberation to not what you have learned, and got to know, but what it is yet that you have to KNOW. However, life school is full of lessons you learn on the way, and it is these very experiences that mould you, it also throws many challenges en route, this is the essence of your evolvement on this planet earth. Value life for what it is, time races past so quickly, the present moments of today will all become tomorrow's memories of yesterday, which becomes your past. Focus and attempt to achieve today and reap the pleasures to come, the dynamic of the energy changes to a feel-good factor, an achievement, you owe it to yourself, and only you can do it- live life with utmost passion, and enjoy the vibrancy, and positiveness of steps you took to initiate those attempts to achieve the objectives of your goal. The only inspiration you need is you, motivation comes from you, how determined are you will give you room for thought? Remember thought is energy that motivates the mind to manipulate the body to that action.

I'm walking my journey, the path may never be straight all the time, but what I have learned and I am still learning, is that the steps I take through life's challenges is what makes me. I'm not just anybody, I am unique, I am my soul, serving my purpose on this planet, I am still here and I am still there, I am everywhere, sometimes my mission takes me on challenges deeper than the heart follows. The ebb and flow of life is a continuous and constant exchange. We are forever learning and imparting lessons. This is school of life, and one can only learn, teach, give, receive in the equilibrium of life. You are never alone on your path; along the way you are continuously encountering other beautiful souls. I am truly humbled, grateful and blessed, and honour each beautiful soul that has crossed paths with me, for without them what purpose would I be fulfilling, what would I be learning and what would I be imparting? We all are a creation of love and divinity. I connect through my soul honouring the souls of all I meet. Each of us are on our own unique journey weaving a beautiful tapestry of our life, with a continuous flow of exchange, connection and equilibrium. This weaving is our life story.

What kind of tapestry are you weaving? The flow of this journey will come to an end one day, when a call home is heard. This very tapestry will be the inventory of your life to Source/Universe/God. It may have taken a lifetime to present your life story, but does it justify to be a breath-taking bestseller when its finished, for that itself is an accomplishment? What you strive for is the drive within you to achieve, accomplish and complete to the utmost perfection within your capabilities.

Journey of Transformation

I am one within as you see, all you see, is all you have

If I am all that I am to you, then this is your acceptance of me

If I am to change, I am still the one within this oneness

Think no different, think no less, think no more

Changes are just a dress rehearsal, camouflaged under the layers is still me

Change is imminent, layers can be removed

Look deep within me and you shall still see me, this is your acceptance of me

Look no further, look no nearer, as you see I am still within me

Changes on the exterior are only to see, as you see the interior is still within

Criticise not, judge not, comment at your will

What you see is what you get, I am one as you see

Look deep within, I am who I am

Always have been and always will be

Chapter 1

EXISTENCE

You are your life force, encapsulate the power of what is within, that is Jewel of all access to reach beyond one's limitations. The reality of the existence is to be in awareness of the presence of all that is. It is a perception of how one perceives of what they assimilate to be.

You are your existence, live in your existence to the term of this existence you have been given one chance, your life in this lifetime! There is no need for competitiveness, you are beyond anything else, you are your ultimate best and are you trying your ultimate best, why the need to compete with ANOTHER, it all starts with oneself, challenges are for one's self for growth and expansion of one's existence, whatever you overcome and you defeat, you then get through, your life force, your existence, once in recognition of this you are in awareness of your abilities and capabilities to overcome and get through.

Tap into this existence of your being to understand to the nature of one's soul. Living is just not adhering to what's around, but reining in to the power of reality of who you really are. Walking the path in a daze does not lift the veils of what you perceive to be. Allow the ego to settle, subside to overcome the presentation of the obstacle one faces that's imminent and restrictive to the vow of one's journey, face it, acknowledge, surrender to overcome to free the shackles of those constraints that so bind you. You cannot simply move, elevate, ascend, descend without the awareness of what is, was, must be.

Be free in the living to experience the joy, not when approaching life's end to free oneself. There is such cliche, how when one completes their earthly soul contract, and takes that transition to experience the thrill and joy of freeing from a vessel that bound them to whatever, whichever constraints that prevented them living an existence. Live your existence in the presence of the now of what is and not what will be. So much is wasted through the weariness of the hum drum of life, that no one is really living it to the freedom of the free flow from within.

There is so much written about when people are nearing end of life of regrets of what they should have done, never had chance to do, whether it's broken relationships, goals, aspirations etc because in amidst of their living they were too consumed into a constraint that restricted a flow or impeded one's journey. This wakeup call is too late to complete, wake up in every presence of the stance of your being, so when one reaches a stage of nearing or completion of life, one can be sure they have fulfilled their wills to the very existence of their being to experience that exact fulfilment.

Don't be a living dead, but arise to live the soul of your being in the existence of that human life you have been graced with!

You are your power, you are your mechanism, you are responsible for driving, walking and navigating your lifepath...only you...you cannot step onto another's life path and take control. Your life ship is navigated by your own control...does one sink or flow with the tide, does one derail from the path, stops and stances the flow. You wouldn't necessarily stop your route mid flow of any journey knowing the consequences or outcomes. Think of it being on a busy freeway/motorway...would you stop mid flow in a journey because you didn't know any better? Imagine the destruction of havoc....everything within everything, has a cause and an effect. Your life is a cause to the effect of the outcome of what you are navigating it to. Power is within that mass of engineering of the mind, body and spirit. Grasp these tools to the adherence of controlling the directive flow of the path of existence, once you tap into the power of this you are in control to experience the thrill, joy and experience of your human existence. Don't wait until it is too late- regrets don't serve a purpose. Life is living in the now, feel it, embrace it, and acknowledge it to recognise who you are in the very presence of each moment that arises. A moment passed becomes the past, a moment that has not arrived is yet far becomes the future, the moment that arises is the power of what it is that you become...that is the stance of your living in the being of the presence in the present. The past cannot serve, it's gone, the future is to come through the thrill of what you experience now to attract the vast of what is yet to come....

May the power of you, always be in alignment to serve you always in alignment of your highest purpose and development as a part of that human evolvement.

Praise be beautiful soul, you are only awake once you realise your worth, and who you are and what your purpose is. Along the way you have lost this purpose, and lost sense of one's self. You are going through life in a pace, biggest challenges are to defeat in all the mind programming you have endured, the way and process you have been programmed in life is to actually take an inventory of one self – Currently is this what is truly making you happy? How do you discover you? Attempt to look within, to recognise the power of you. Your discovery of you itself will be empowering. If you are lost you are just plodding along without really living in the moment or the presence of your being. Awaken and be in awareness to understand life of who you are. Until you truly understand the core of yourself, there is no value or recognition of purpose. Life just passes by us without us pausing to take those moments and it's about connecting yet we are so dis connected, but one day, when you come to that point of dawning or realisation you become awake, and then you act upon that awakening. Only you are the masterpiece of your own life, and only you can make that carving of your destiny, and this destiny is what is weaved into this tapestry, and when you look back on this tapestry, you would love to think your creator views a spectacular weaving you did here on this journey on earth, the school of life. It doesn't matter about understanding anything, other than understanding YOU, who you are and what your mission is, then that dawning of that realisation of who you truly are is very significant and powerful above and beyond anything. The recognition of I. I AM, Oneself, Me, Myself.

One morning at 3.33am, I was tossing and turning, and eventually awoke as it was more than likely something was being revealed from my higher self. There definitely was some nudging going on. Heart resonance is what I got. It is often the hum drum of day to day living, that we are so focused on the mind, body and spirit, yet the heart is often overlooked. This chamber is where the mystery and myriad of life, living and embodiment of wholesome resides. We need to acknowledge, respect and delve into this essence of wholesome to find the peaceful state and more importantly love of who we are. We berate ourself so much throughout life due to conditioning. The oneself is where we need to honour ourselves to find the real purpose of what, who and purpose of oneself. If we cannot answer these 3 questions, we really are not living the role of who we are and the purpose of our being here. We are just allowing life to pass without really immersing it. The heart is the one organ that is responsible for our functioning, yet it also impacts the most attacks through pain from embedded emotions and feelings, that arise from stored deep traumas. These emotions and feelings, have been subjected to painful episodes and experiences, and become wounded scars that are never given an opportunity to heal, but remain closed. This chamber is where the wholeness of the universe exists, and resides, yet we often look elsewhere. Up above and beyond. The connection is within oneself yet this aspect of all is so dis connected. We are equipped with a highly intelligent system, but don't know how to efficiently and smoothly operate this. However, on technical issues, we know the reasons, for example, if anything is not working or flowing as it should be, your car, TV, iron, washing machine, PC, etc we try and identify why it is malfunctioning in order to rectify it. Yet concerning our vessel, we attempt to just suppress, and suppress to later, it either manifesting as disease, or ailment that requires medical intervention. There is no need for any of this as it's all self-inflicted, the self has a powerful magnificent system that just is not utilised to operate in accordance of free will of being. The brain is the power centre and your heart is the source of fuel to run it. The fuel to feed this is LOVE, the flame of divinity is extinguished through all programming of society. This is not your free will of who you are. Yet you are functioning through physical level as in blood circulation being pumped throughout the body through your pumping chamber, but the spiritual ethos of one's being is in slumber or dead. Life is so exuberant and joyful until the age of seven, as the consciousness is free of the constraints of programming and conditions. We only have to look at children, they are the perfect example of free will and living until the nature of imbedded rules, programmes and conditions set in and start to either take effect then and there or stored for later.

You have the power to set yourself free to just be, to discover that you have found yourself, and life then suddenly becomes joyful to live, and that is where you find the purpose of your being. Until you can define this, you are not existing but just drifting from day to day. Find yourself, you are there and it all becomes so effortless and all your needs are met with such efficiency at your free will disposal. Everything is within reach, it's all there, we haven't come here to live a life of suffering, which is all self-inflicted, but the actual joy of life is suppressed so deep.

Our soul incarnation has chosen to come here for an experience, it's already embedded in love, and the experience of the eternal realms from home in heaven, but arriving on the earth realms this wholesome, the epitome of love is harshly suppressed due to these earthly constraints. It need not be impacted or subjected to this harshness, that it closes off and the system fails to operate in the mechanism and functionality it arrived in. Find your heart resonance to start the engine, to immerse and embrace the love, and you will have it all and more through discovering you-the lost soul.

Walk the path that has been bestowed upon you. Sometimes it is the most difficult challenges through such extenuating circumstances that we find our way. We have to endure those shadows of darkness, often referred to as the dark night of the soul, to get through the passage to the beam of light.

Often, we succumb to the weariness, and give up or in too easily. Reflect upon your stance to the presence of where one is already. You may have already fought your way continuously to the point just to just give up, to not be aware of your present stance, just to block and hinder what awaits. The glorification and wonder are speculative; however, the gratification is the freedom and replenishment, the divine nectar of which the soul seeks. Knowing thyself through this deepest inhabitant of thyself is the liberation, one cannot be living if they feel awakened to the light. The doorway is only but within reach, the reality of existence is so programmed in a matrix of illusion that one adheres to. This entanglement of what one deems is life, is but an illusion. Once the realisation of one's existence is realised there is far more to the vast horizon that awaits...wisdom is embedded to reveal that knowledge, but one has also got to trust. It's like being in a maze, and finding your way out. Struggle becomes a part of that imprint if you so allow it, if you just let go, and be what you feel is lost within oneself is where you will find your way out. This is the exhilaration of that entanglement. The same applies to the vessel that allows the mind to control by such programmes. Unfold, untangle what is not useful or impedes your evolution, set the focus to achieve the ultimate enlightenment to the existence of oneself. If you truly set yourself free, you recognise the worth of liberation of your soul.

You merely recognise this aspect of your worth and purpose here. Yet you question your journey, your hardship laboured upon thyself by the laborious programmes that have falsified or lulled you into just being a living dead. Live from your heart, awaken the mind to declutter, clear and create the joyous art of what the soul needs to thrive. Truth be said you are not your thoughts, feelings or emotions, you are far beyond this. Throughout life this gift of incarnation is suppressed from living due to the moulding of the expectations of what society deems is appropriate. These walls are crumbling, the speck of the wondrous light is illuminated through the cracks, this is the way through.

Living is the right to the war of such darkness to have fought to obtain the light of one's very existence. When you descend the tangles of such ferocity of this darkness, you have won the war. It is not far out of reach but in duality of your existence. As I am writing this my, I AM presence of higher self has channelled "We walk amongst you, yet you perceive that what you receive or channel is something far beyond attaining, unless one is in the embodiment of spiritual ethos or enlightenment! Live now, don't wait until it is far too late."

Never regret, because this too suppress the soul of not obtaining one's path of existence. There can never be regrets if you take hold of the reins of your being NOW! It starts and ends with YOU... you can orchestrate that map to navigate your way through to your destination of your being. It is the not knowing you feel lost, even the lost will ways find a way through, with a determination to see one's self through to the other side. If you give up attempt after attempt you have failed not thyself but to reach and feel that what frees you, is so far beyond what constricts oneself. Freedom of the soul is not through death, but awakening of oneself.

The existence of what is around you is only matter, dense matter... this is not an existence just suppression. The soul can exist on many dimensions past the current illusion. You have the choice to win the war of your survival, or give up in the dense matter of non-existent living dead. Obey not the commands of what must be, but of what is far beyond this and much more. You can define your existence as that purpose because then you have found you, the lost soul. Blessed are those that live life of the true reality of what one is and not one becomes!

A journey back home to the unleashing of the incarnated soul is too late of no return. Live now to cease the exhilaration of what you are missing. Don't allow the cracks of the crumbling walls be plastered to deny you, to the horizon beyond the dimension of your stance now....these specks of light are showing you the way....

You question, yet you know the answers. They are within you once you find yourself. Make an attempt to truly recognise your magnificence imbedded in this cloak of density. The sparkle and zest of living was fun and joyous until you were programmed into obeying the obedience structure of programme of what is needed to stall your growth and not evolve to that aspect of you, the joyous fun free-living spirit. Tap into reveal this aspect of oneself to fully appreciate and be in gratitude of the opportunity to find your free spirit.

This part of you is the very creation of your purpose here, find your way through this mass and you have found you. Blessed are those that really recognise who they truly are! You are just not someBODY, or noONE but your soul. In this vessel of yours is the most precious commodity, asset of existence. Find your connection through your heart, the heartbeat is to the rhythm of the universe. It exists within you.

Today Declare: *I AM a free spirit, I set myself free from any limitations. My freedom is my liberation, I gracefully move forward in the cycle of life, the constant stream of the ups and downs, of giving & receiving. I arise like a Phoenix from any turbulence. I am loving my existence; I am consistently thankful and grateful for even the smallest things provide huge dividends!*

CREATION

I AM, a beautiful soul. Feel and merge into the existence of your creation, imprint the energy of this lifetime with all the love from your heart, the shining light from your soul, the wisdom from your spirit, illuminate and enlighten all you can, to transform your expansion above and beyond. What is in the here and now, will count towards all the tomorrow's and beyond. You are in control of this journey, utilise the power of your creation and see what unfolds. Enjoy your life one magnificent step at a time on this vast planet, we are all here for a purpose to fulfil our life mission, and so much more. May all the days of your creation be showered with tenfold eternal blessings and abundance.

So it is, and so mote it be!

Chapter 2

FLOW

The line is never straight, a flow has a curve. The directional flow is either up and down, in and out. Representation of one's journey can be of the highs (up) and lows (down), one going off (out) one's directional flow, on their journey to either experience another aspect of lesson/s or overcoming challenges or obstacles, then joining (in) that continuous flow. Your path will continue as long as that last ounce of breath in your body.

The adaptation to one's flow of life is release, let go and surrender to the constriction of what is to what will be. The stance of any presence has to be free will of any constraints. There is a directional flow of all matter be it on a human level or planetary level. The earth planet rotates to movement for flow, the sun, the moon rises and sets as does the tide of oceans rises and recedes. The seasons changes too. One wouldn't necessarily plunge into an ocean at high tide for a swim, or necessarily sun bathe with winter clothes or vice versa without knowing the constraints of impeding restriction of flow.

Living in embodiment of just being is free flow come what may. The duty of obligation to oneself is always through choice that becomes the outcome. To foresee the outcome is the desired effort one exerts through their choice.

Anything in life does not just happen, it results from what the input is to receive the output. If happiness is derived from the thrill of the thoughts one perceives, then surely the action needs to be implemented to achieve that desired effect to come into fruition, to then actually experience that exact thrill.

Thoughts and emotions are driven by the mind, surely if the mind is the control box, it is in consistent autopilot because it knows everything from set programmes.

It is only to a certain point, consistent patterns serve whether it's habits or behaviours, but in time they become mundane. To serve oneself to the highest vibrational flow is to live freely and ride that flow joyously.

"Watch your thoughts, they become your words; watch your words, they become your actions; watch your actions, they become your habits; watch your habits, they become your character; watch your character, it becomes your destiny."
— **Lao Tzu**

Every day is that bonus of living and experiencing another day. I am happy because I am choosing to be. In this happiness I find my peace, in this peace I find the resolute of all that needs to be. It doesn't matter about the a's & b's or the xyz...just simply being in the presence of each moment is the power. Be in your power, you are the reins of your life, the control box maybe programmed to be in autopilot.

The thrill of living is the excitement and passion of experiencing living, not the continuous mundane of set patterns derived from set programmes because they are always just momentary.

There is a duality and equilibrium in every aspect of everything, the masculine, the feminine, the sun, the moon, day, night, happiness, sadness. Death, birth, inhalation of breath the exhalation of breath, hot, cold. The up the down, the in and out.

The dark (night) the light (day). There is a balance and equilibrium to all in everything. The sync is never out.

Your own vessel and mechanism knows it's fight or flight mode? It will react to what is presented. If one's body temperature drops that body will work hard to reset to the set temperature required for its optimal efficiency to work, the same applies for the opposite, if it rises it automatically sets to work to derive a balance within, also releasing the emotions that's allows you to react to those thoughts to bring about the action to sustain or net the required balance.

The flow of a life journey takes so many twists and turns, regardless the flow will always continue its destination, until the length of that journey comes to an end. We sometimes get so consumed in resistance fighting the flow, that we forget the experience of living in the moment, therefore missing many vital moments that could have eased oneself amidst any struggles. Living becomes difficult if one cannot understand how to live. Your only alive if you can encapsulate any one moment, even just a brief pause.

In every moment of living, you will have the past- yesterday, the present- today, and the future- tomorrow. Every day you are presented with options and choices, the past cannot be changed its happened. Today you are in control, and tomorrow hasn't even arrived, but it's an option to start all over again. We are always surrounded in a power of three, there are three days- yesterday, today, and tomorrow, always three choices! Three is associated with trinity, (mind, body, soul) therefore in each stance we have the opportunity of creation which is your body, manifestation which is your mindset, and evolution which is your soul growth. Feel in the empowerment of your being today, for you have control today. There is no time like the present, take control and rise freely in your power...yesterday is the past, that door has closed, tomorrow your future awaits, but today you can make it happen! Allow the power of positivity in your present stance surge through your soul, freeing you to dance to the destiny of your wonderful path ahead. Live in the present, in the now, this is the energy circuit currently wired up to the universal frequency. The signal is live in the present, yesterday it has disconnected and tomorrow is not yet live, but you have the option to attract your desires in the present connection so it is forthcoming in all the tomorrows.

How you make your day is ultimately the choices you make to set the flow, and the outcome. We alone are responsible for any outcome or predicament, me, you, us and them doesn't control it, it is YOU and you alone, almost allowing your mind to accept that you alone have control and responsibility. I always use the term me, myself and I are going to make today remarkable.

Each new dawn is a new day, no point resisting it, it's here, it starts with YOU!!! Feel the gratitude of awaking and taking your breath. Don't think about yesterday, today, or tomorrow. Just become aware of just your presence and the present moment. Encapsulate just in that sacred moment, nothing else matters just you, come what may, be aware of the presence of your stance, and those moments itself will create the reality of your day. You are a powerful being, shine in your presence. At each dawn of new rising, create your day, and as the sunsets, feel the gratitude of your day and your presence.

Set your positive intentions to allow all the good to gravitate towards you. You are in control of your life path; you are responsible for your journey...your destination...so make it a good one! Make the ride an exciting, joyous and blessed one. Upon reflection you will realise the route was even better than your expectation.

Positive thoughts will energise you, your mind and your body, the negative vibe will create sombre energy. You are responsible for what you put in your mindset to activate the body to react and follow those patterns.

Your thoughts are energy, this energy can flow in the direction of your intention by manoeuvring, and manipulating these thoughts for the outcome, thereby creating a positive flow away from a negative vibe. You are in control of the gearbox (your mind) What unfolds will be with the way you flowed.

A journeys flow or route sometimes is never a straight line, destruction on a path can be presented by forks, this doesn't mean the journey has come to an end, it's a temporary stall or pause to divert off your path and then to recommence.

My journey's flow was disrupted. The year 2016 for me was a catalyst of the lows, as oppose to the highs in a major way, with many catastrophic moments. Reflecting back, I had every opportunity to rein my life back in, if I was in control, yet I continued to be controlled blindly by events at each turn. Having carved a great business as a Holistic practitioner, I was immensely proud and very grateful of my gifts as a healer. I felt truly honoured, and blessed as well as worthy to be talented in this field. By the grace of God doing God's mission felt very joyous and exuberant. For me as an individual it was of a great service, and an honour to another human being, to help and assist them on their journey, freeing them from the depths of darkness to the elevation of light. To touch another's life to blossom fully in their human self, spiritually, mentally, emotionally and physically has got to be the best reward than any amount of wealth. The abundance of feedback from each client was an honour and humbling validation of services rendered.

I never allowed myself to succumb to weakness of any kind. I was a strong, positive, vibrant successful woman. I had a very driven work ethos and achieved tasks and aims. All this was going to change beyond my control. In January 2016 whilst meditating in a group session, I was overcome with sadness and lots of tears, literally broke down. I apologised to the group that this was so unlike me, obviously in hindsight my higher self was bringing it all up. I was reassured by friends and fellow colleagues it probably ascertained to bottled emotions of losing my only child (daughter) to her forthcoming marriage, later in August that year. This felt apt and I took it in my stride, and it made sense, it was like a grieving process, on the positive, I was reassured I was actually gaining a son in law, this helped to null the emotions.

The wedding was a blast, the joy and happiness didn't last too long. My dearest younger brother collapsed at the pre wedding celebrations, and within a week he suddenly, and unexpectedly passed away. When I look back, the tears and sadness, I had felt in that meditation in January, were actually the loss of my brother to the eternal realms of gods kingdom. My higher self was already preparing me. Heartbreak far outweighed the happiness of the wedding, and it seemed a distant memory in those seven days. I took time out from my healing modalities to grieve, as well as to recover from major surgery that followed a couple of months later. I had to take of three months off work, although full recovery was forecasted as six months. Fate had something else in store and decided to step in February 2017, my father became ill with prediction to not lasting beyond months, to surviving a major surgery, then a continuous cycle of predicaments of not lasting to pulling through, coming on the other side of pre-arranged palliative care. The cycle continued from the fighting spirit within him, this exceptional man, my darling "poppy". I always referred dad to either popsie or poppy. To the astonishment of all, this warrior had far exceeded 9 lives of a cat, and astounded the medical profession each time.

September 2018, fate had another plan in store for me. Like a bolt of lightning out of nowhere my dearest mom, had a major stroke! So, the path in my journey divided into a fork. I took on caring duties full on, that lasted four long years with poppy, and another four, caring for my mother who incidentally had another stroke December 2019. So, my sole life role, and purpose had extended into roles of nursing, caring, cooking, cleaning, chauffeuring, hospital, clinic, duties etc and so the endless list went on. My life was not mine anymore, and who's fault was that-MINE- I lost control of me. Astonishingly, in the process of all this, the strength and tenacity within me arose to all challenges. Each day I managed to get through with adrenaline, by nightfall I was exhausted. I was just thankful I was always blessed with energy for another day. My parent's healthcare was at a detriment if I was not functioning. Being such a perfectionist to every detail of their healthcare needs I just couldn't entrust this to anyone, as in Carers or social care.

Every day we awaken to another day, and just take it as granted, and mindlessly forget our gratitude, of what a blessing itself is to be alive. Today the present is another day to start over. Reborn again like a rising phoenix through the ashes, freeing yourself from the shackles of any suppression. Allow each day forth to become a daily mantra of Carpe diem. Each morning is a start to a new day, come what may, the morning will come out of the dark night through light of the sun as it rises. You will arise from the slumber of the night, the mind will be stirring the awakening signals, before the eyes open, just breathe, it's a moment of carpe diem for you to seize the opportunity to start over again.

I recall posting this quote of mine on my social media, to update all those beautiful souls who followed me, friends, clients, colleagues and likeminded souls.

"Good morning to all you beautiful souls, new day, new month and very significant it is for me (my birth month!) It's been a long time, and it's time to recommence, and reconnect from this arduous journey that is still ongoing. This turbulent path has been ongoing. What a year! I endured 2 personal losses one of happiness, my only child, my beautiful daughter to marriage, followed by sadness, my younger brother who left his earthly incarnation. Then followed my major surgery, which I had not fully recovered from, to be thrown into the depths of ill health of a very special beautiful spiritual soul...my life, my everything, my hero,...my DAD. Whilst I may not control the outcome, it is still an ongoing roller coaster. I trust and accept that all that unfolds is what God's plan is, but for now I take today as the first step to bring me, my life, my journey back into focus. Lessons in life are what makes you! and what doesn't break you, only makes you stronger.

Gratitude and blessings for each lesson we are endowed with, from this "School of Life" journey, every experience is a part of our growth and evolvement. Sometimes the most difficult, and painful lessons are the deepest and darkest challenging experiences in life, however prayer and hope gives positivity, but TIME often overlooked suddenly becomes too precious".

This diversion on my emotional journey took a lot longer than I had anticipated. Sometimes it's all about "trust & divine will" whilst I may not have had the control on the journey and its outcome. I most certainly attempted to take charge and ownership on mine. In my mindset and heart, I set the intention that my comeback, which I used as a mantra "The comeback is always stronger than the setback" Diversions may come and go, but the route always continues on this magnificent destination "The Earth Plane" who said being a human was easy!

I AM the mystery in this life striving to solve it...Only when we realise the flow of our journey, the path to a destination...do we truly wake up, the mystery itself is resolved. We are all on a spectacular journey on the earth planes...LIFE…value and enjoy each sacred moment. A moment will come & go but the memory of this will be etched for a lifetime.

Today Declare: *I welcome the abundance of cosmic blessings into this greatest mystery...LIFE...Live it, breathe it, flow with it, unfold it to a beautiful revelation of human existence!*

PRESENCE

I AM, immersed in the NOW as this is the presence I can either make this a good day or a bad day, the choice is mine in this moment that reflects the outcome I choose to overcome and rise above any weakness Surrender, I will not no matter how severe the temptation For there is no power like the one I have in this moment in my presence

So it is, and so mote it be!

Chapter 3

CHALLENGES

Trust and believe in yourself. Any challenge is only a test of inner strength, a part of your growth, believe in you, and you truly recognise your self- worth. What matters is just being, in the presence of all that is...finding you is the ultimate true completeness, in the wholeness of this vastness. YOU are your power, shine your light, illuminate your path, this is your journey, all that you are, and all that you become, is truly within you and always has been. You are in your true power through each positive action and word. Own your power, feel your power, resonate in the mighty "I AM" presence. Your life, your choices, your decisions create your destiny. Believe this and believe the results you create!

Life itself can present so many challenges, sometimes it can be very overwhelming, and feels like you are swallowed in the tide and current of any circumstances that arise, despite focusing on attempting to be positive and trying to rise above it. Many times, I questioned how as a holistic practitioner can I possibly advocate and preach positive steps in the amidst of going through all this. But I guess it's that part of our human tenacity or part that comes into play, this is our emotional body, and you know what sometimes you have to succumb to that part, however there is also a need to be affirmative with oneself, because again when one constantly plays and replays the adverse negative pattern stemming from whatever circumstances are unfolding, you can easily allow yourself to be programmed into creating the reality of that negative behaviour or pattern. So, one has to apply discernment relating that situation.

Challenges are what makes you, never be defeated by them or weakened. This is the making of you, how you evolve and shape as your being. Sometimes we can be overcome by the challenge at hand, but how would you ever learn if you did not experience the task. How can you come out on the other side? Only you are responsible for getting through it, overcoming something, or learning something. Sometimes we have to face our shadows like it or not.

It does not matter what life throws at us. What is important is how we pick ourselves up. For that itself is the strength within each of us, challenges are not a part of our struggles, but a momentous recognition of our growth. Look at where you are today, and count all your blessings. Abundance is all that you are, and all that is around and within you. Only when we are truly grateful, we magnetise and attract more. As I am writing this, I energetically send a smile from my heart to touch the core of your soul, because you are doing great!

Well, I certainly was moved beyond limitations. The Universe had something in store for me that exceeded my expectations! I was presented with 4 challenges, that I somehow resisted on my human level. My only child's wedding, meant to be the happiest of times with so many happy memories, instead was a period of grieving following a loss of a beautiful soul....my younger brother. This occurred within 7days from the wedding. I did not envisage this journey, endured I did. A huge part of me regressed to all the human emotions it presented, then I had to face the prospect of losing my dad. If that wasn't enough! My dearest mother deteriorated rapidly on a downward decline, from not coping with the loss of her beloved soul mate, her husband. It was traumatic enough dealing with the shock of losing her youngest son, which she never got over.

I attempted to take baby steps back into the routine of reality, mainly due to the immense love, support, kindness, words and compassion I received from all friends and clients, for that I am eternally in gratitude. It gave me the courage to embrace fresh start and new beginnings...from the depths of despair I found peace and love, from the depths of darkness I found my way through the guiding light. From a spiritual and divine perspective, I was put through these paces for a reason, and I made it through! Sometimes it's not what you know, but what you are capable of, the potential of all that you are is within you. They will prod you from time to time, I am eternally grateful for this nudging, something new experienced from a lot of help from above!

My mantra:

"Clearing and releasing the past, that no longer serves my highest good, embracing my way forward to all new beginnings. Shedding the old self, making way for new change, directions and transformation. Through the darkness comes the infinite light with new possibilities in perfect alignment of my antenna to Source/God/Universe in the presence of here and now. I am truly blessed and grateful for all that was and all that is coming and so it is"

It's 4.04am- (sign of spiritual awakening and determination for current situation, surrounded by the angelic realms that bring forth peace of mind and joy of heart).

I have been awoken and being given the word compassion:

Allow yourself to have compassion for thyself. Whatever plagues one mind, needs to just slow the pace, observe and release. Sometimes what is not obvious in the presence of time, is because you are oblivious. The effervescent of life may not truly transpire to the state of one's expectations because they are yet not ready. It's timing of patience and perseverance, what may not be evident yet, does not mean it's not happening, it's availability is timed per se, when it is ready. The despondency of yielding to one's expectations needs to acknowledge and bring forth the compassion towards oneself.

Sometimes haste delivers the opposite of the desired expectations, allow yourself with high regard of trusting the outcome. All always falls into place as is required, in perfect timing. The now is already orchestrated in the optimum order of divine timing, not evident per se on human level of timing. Trust the situation... the outcome of the solution is resolution.

In haste the desired objective of any goal is superseded to that of one's comprehension, bring forth the compassion to oneself that the attainment of realisation may not be evident as yet, however it does not mean it's not happening. All is in due course. The destruction of the mind can become turmoiled with mixed filtration of thoughts and messages, causing oneself apprehension of anxiety unnecessarily. Don't be in disbelief, and rush. Life is to pace your way through, believe in the reality of just the presence to acquire what one may deem what their goal is, for that to then come into manifestation. Observe through compassion, have faith, trust and believe. This is the hardest work, for the deliverance of the outcome.

Oneself through compassion sets the perception of requirements, through consciousness in perfect harmony of alignment, the human level necessitates the steps to acquire the right steps to achieve the desired result. In balance the outcome will be the desired outcome.

As always, I am in deepest gratitude for this wonderful channelling; please may I ask who assists me this morning?

Again, I am informed have compassion to what has been given, time is patience for any revelation. By gaining what you feel you need, will it make it any less or more important. You are fully aware yet oblivious. The wisdom has always been there, yet you have chosen not to tap or delve into the deeper innermost consciousness. You are ready now…again we repeat observe through compassion, have faith, trust and love that belief of the reality of the true identity of who you are. Not just a human being, but a soul incarnated into a vessel. The deliverance of such wisdom and knowledge from eons is birthed now through such dialect. The importance of this deliverance is pertinent to who may assist. Your spiritual team is always gathered in support of you facilitating the path for oneself and all.

We take leave now…

I give my huge gratitude and love for all your guidance, love and support on this journey "I am deeply grateful Thank you!"

Fear can be a big challenge in itself, it is so misunderstood. The most frightening and fearful experience can leave a dramatic impact on oneself. Take for example Friday 13th, many are programmed into believing that Friday the 13th is an unlucky day, NOT…it is all but a misconception of belief system, therefore you create the reality of what you hear around you, been brought up to believe. Many look forward to a Friday with excitement, as it's the end of the week, and it welcomes the weekend, yet when it just so happens to be the 13th, then fear rears its ugliness up …so what!! Numerologically, and spiritually the number 13 is not an unlucky number, it signifies energy, inspiration, motivation, love and compassion. 1+3= 4, which signifies "being" connection of mind, body and spirit, stability and strength on solid foundations of values and beliefs. I LOVE the number 13 and my life path number is 4, so I am embracing the energies of magic already.

Sometimes the very thing in front of our vicinity, is the one we are most ignorant towards. Any provoked thoughts, feelings and emotions can also be there as reminders to look deeper, as the answer is just there. However, we choose to shake, shrug or dismiss it. This is undeniably allowing oneself the opportunity to delve deeper with clarity for a direction, that then should become a focus to attain a result.

Conquer any fear that you may have arising by recognising and deciphering the word fear itself to:

Freedom- freeing yourself from the attachment and gaining freedom from the situation.

Empowerment – taking your power back to control situation and being immersed in your own empowerment.

Assertive – Once you gain empowerment, you naturally feel confident to assert yourself in whatever situation arises.

Release- You feel joyful and excited when a shift occurs from a negative situation to a powerful positive perspective, that is your release.

Our beautiful vessel is a 4-body energy system, and I have abbreviated this to **PEMS**. So, P= physical, E=emotional, M= mental and S= spiritual.

When you are in fear of a challenge or situation, strategize from the perspective of applying PEMS from a positive ethos. This can be done in any order that you desire, there is no right or wrong way. The challenge is to get through, and overcome the situation or circumstance of fear!

<u>Physical</u> sense - Fight, Effort, Attitude, Reviving
<u>Emotional</u> sense -Forgive, Emotions, Attempt, Resistance
<u>Mental</u> sense– Fearless, Energy, Activate, Renew

Spiritual sense- Faith, Embrace, Align, Rebalance

Behaviour says a lot from the body language you display.

From your physical sense- **fight** to overcome the weakness, put the **effort** in, to strive forward with the right **attitude,** to **reviving** yourself. **(fear)**

From your emotional sense - **forgive** yourself, and another for putting you in the scenario you are facing, recognise the **emotions** presented, and **attempt** to overcome them without **resistance**. **(fear)**

From your mindset, your mental sense -be **fearless** in your thoughts, the **energy** you feed them produces the emotions that connect to the feelings you are perceiving, adapt to **activate**, and encourage positive thoughts, to **renew** and become aligned with the intention for what you seek. **(fear)**

Therefore, from a spiritual sense - you have **faith** in yourself and capabilities, to **embrace** and **align** yourself in centredness, so you continuously **rebalance** against all odds from any obstacles. **(fear)**

So now your fear in each of your four-body system becomes the positives.

PEMS

Negative	POSITIVE TRANSLATION			
	Physical	Emotional	Mental	Spiritual
F	Fight	Forgive	Fearless	Faith
E	Effort	Emotions	Energy	Embrace
A	Attitude	Attempt	Activate	Align
R	Reviving	Resistance	Renew	Rebalance

Kim Dhaliwal

How I applied the PEMS strategy to a personal experience.

The year 2020 (covid pandemic) will go down in history for a huge amount of the population worldwide for varying reasons, a year that each individual will recall for years to come.

My own experience was that of a personal loss of my dearest father, who I always referred to as "poppy or popsie" and also another very close family relative. It was a time when lockdown rules were being semi relaxed. Poppy was dying and inevitably it was going to happen someday. The sudden death of my first cousin, came out like a bolt of lightning unexpectedly. It hit me extremely hard, we had grown up together, and also, he had a young family but what hit me the most, was I never got the opportunity to say my goodbye when it was the funeral. I didn't expect to get invited due to covid restrictions on numbers, and I was mindful of those rules, and I also had to respect the close family wishes. My grievance was I wasn't even invited to just wait outside the house. I was totally dissolute and on the same token it felt like a hurtful insult that I was not allowed to be invited just for a brief 10minutes to the family home when the funeral cortege of my first cousin came home. For me that was like a nail in the heart (not in the coffin) pardon the pun!

I had to accept it, even though I did not take well to this, and consequently allowed this information to cause havoc with my energy system through my emotional body and my mental body. I tried to reason with the outcome of what I was feeling but no it just didn't ease my understanding of why....

I really did allow myself to entertain those disrupting thoughts that totally messed with my energy system. It was only later that evening I decided only a long walk was going to shake me out of this negative humdrum, and by releasing my physical body from this havoc! The long walk of 1-hour 45minutes, and the music in my earphones totally eased, helped me make peace with the situation, to a point I just reasoned and accepted that I was never going to allow myself to feel like that again with anyone, from anyone, and to anyone. The focus was to be in oneness, be in the vibration of the energy when you are connected to source, universe and being in this flame of divinity where love diffused any effect of the affect of a or any situation. This was rebalancing my spiritual body.

PATH

I AM, walking my journey, the path is never straight all the time, but what I learn as I take my steps through my challenges, this is what makes me. I'm not just anybody, I am my soul serving my purpose on this planet. I salute all those that I meet along the way, each beautiful being in constant exchange of giving and receiving, lessons gained, lessons imparted, lessons blessed with experiences, for this is evolvement. Blessed I feel always in every way as I realise our paths were meant to cross. God always has a plan, reasons only known to him, to put certain individuals on a path to meet at any one given time. In abundance I feel for there is no void of emptiness or isolation but a constant stream of learning. I judge not as all is one, for each is in the image of God's creation that I acknowledge. I am to them as they are to me, this is what the human race is!

So it is, and so mote it be!

Life is your journey, if you are not chosen to be a part of another's, then one should still continue to flow the path of their journey and not of another. To invite fear in unnecessarily you become stalled in being stuck in that specific challenge, life does not flow because ultimately you alone, are allowing a predicament to control the very circumstance. You are in a sink or swim situation; the tide can engulf you or you can ride the wave of the current, and choose with determination and stamina to get through it. Believe it or not the feeling on the other side of this, you have survived the turmoil of war you inflicted upon your personal self.

Personal experiences are the making of you, and not the destruction, although some can choose the latter, but again this results down to choice, always mind over matter. Your mind is a powerful tool how it influences the body will ultimately display the course of actions you take. Something to think about...

Having said that I was strong to the point of the following morning. I gave into the commands of the mind, as it likes to control if we listen to it, and I did because I started to question the events of the whole dilemma yet again! One's own self-control has to come into play by actually saying STOP!!!! this ends now. I can choose to either win or succumb to the saboteur of thoughts, feelings and emotions. So that's what I did, if they don't care why should I? Sometimes no matter how strong you are, you will succumb to that humanness of you, the part that comes to play into the reality. Apply the PEMS and SNAP out of it!

The purpose of your life is to fulfil your mission, so your soul feels complete. Define the depths of YOU and your purpose, and all will unfold as it needs to. Who said human evolvement was anything but easy...applaud yourself for the many challenges you have faced to where you are today, these very life experiences and lessons are the moulding of you! If you have not defined your purpose.

Today Declare: I serve my life plan with the most impressionable imprint of my life story....I am the bestseller of a lifetime...this is my purpose and I am driven by it!

YOUR STORY

I AM, in flow of my story. It starts with a beginning that is destiny, and concludes with an ending that is fate. It does not matter how the journey is flowing, being part of it, is what counts! When you let go and allow the story to unfold, it is only then you truly become aware of the lessons you are experiencing. The good, the bad, the ugly, the beautiful, the happy, the sad as well as the joyous and painful ones, they are all are part of the verse and chapter. Allow your life to be a bestseller of your existence. Set the intentions of beauty & love into today and all the coming days ahead, every second, minute, hour. Know that we all are truly magnificent beings in this manual of life.

So it is, and so mote it be!

Chapter 4

AWAKEN TO YOUR PRESENCE

In the essence of beauty all is hidden, as sometimes revealing all of the glory can be breathtakingly deniable. It is difficult as it is with the pace of life, the hum drums of the awareness is heightened to a level that one cannot exist beyond. The importance is-one should not be limited just because that is the "norm" There is no norm…life is free or so should be of constraints…the joy is stripped away, harshness is lured in.

What should be so simple in simplicity of life is far beyond that one cannot escape from. The reality is there is far much more to be obtained than abstained. Let's say tiredness would evoke weariness, yet that itself is dialecting a message, we are not one within but so detached, not interconnected but disconnected. This weariness is not joyful, it's a slow detachment. The vessel is withdrawing, sheltering. The art of living is closing inwards, there isn't a will to feel free. Slumber inwards is losing all those precious moments.

We are blessed with each day, as nothing is guaranteed. Yet we are not fulfilling each day to any potential, but slumbering forth. Days are presented for a purpose, nights are presented for the specific of honouring your vessel for rest and recuperation, the purpose of optimisation of your internal system, upgraded, nurtured, repaired in preparation for whatever unfolds for your tomorrow's. There is plain ignorance deemed upon ourselves when we are not operative in a fully functional state. Life sometimes just becomes an autopilot, this isn't living or experiencing the very essence of you, and the purpose you are here for? What legacy are you imprinting to leave? Is it an impressionable one for a life that just lived, a superficial one, or a remarkable official one. Because you only get one chance, you can't come back and re live it or change it. The granted opportunities are now, once they pass, they become missed opportunities. Don't subject yourself to flow in a slumber but more to an awakened state of being. As the saying goes "Health is your wealth" when you have so much of it, you are aligned and interconnected. The dis connection is the opposite, a decline, a poor state of being. Which would you prefer to be in? Your energy system is controlled by you, is it lacking or is it fuelled.

Life isn't about this and that, him or her, them or me, it's solely you, your stance, your recognition of acceptance of who you truly are. Nothing else should really matter, as it's only a gathering of matter that you have collected that doesn't really mean anything. It is just matter of nothing, no value to it. Only you are responsible for considering it, then subjecting yourself to the consequences that flow from it.

Be free, just flow of such constraints, the alteration of the frequency changes the vibration of your existence and the exuberance of just being becomes unconditional, no conditions, no pressures, just you in free flow. This is living, in the flow of accordance and will. Not fast paced, neither slow paced, just cruise flow.

High pressure, low pressure, high tides, low tides, high winds, low winds. Even in nature there is an equilibrium of balance. Just look at water, it will only flow one way, not stop and flow backwards. So why as humans, we don't flow our journey onwards, in forward motion to progress, not stop, pause or impede our journey. We either never let the past go, it becomes a habitual pattern of a consistent backward visiting routine, or just stagnantly become a squatter in it. Today is just that: To do, day, = the presence of now, to achieve, to accomplish, and flourish forward. Embrace TODAY in gratitude, yesterday's battles are of the past, today you have control, the future is another day.

Today Declare: *I am in charge from this moment, this stance, I am powerfully equipped to overcome at my free will. As your day ends reflect with happiness in your heart, mind and the soul. May today and all your days be blessed and good, it starts and ends with you, make it count! and when tomorrow arrives, another opportunity to start all over again.*

Awakening is to be in the awareness of the reality within, and around you in every presence of time. We can go through life being in a slumber. As a spiritual and holistic human being, I thought I was awakened, upon reflection there were certain times that I was in a slumber, the reality was, I was not happy in certain areas of my life, yet I carried on because there was always a ton of excuses to justify why the happiness, contentment or finding peace with the predicament of each or any circumstances I was encased in, didn't come.

It is not through the lack of attempting and failing but picking yourself up and re attempting. How else does one learn? The drive of ingenuity is within you, tap into this reservoir. The self-saboteur within you is not the achiever. There is a façade to what we perceive as being attaining to something, when in reality we are far from it, the exterior of you is indifference to the interior within. The projection is the task in mindset, the action taken determines the outcome, the result portrays the emotion-success (positive) or failure (negative).

How will you ever know what it is that you are afraid off, if you don't question it. You need to solve what it is, that is preventing you from moving forward. Is it rejection, success, failure, are you seeking approval? Delve into what is arising within and question yourself further and assimilate the reasons to get an understanding. Does your ego (lower self) win or your higher self?

Your lower ego will always present temptations of negativity or diversions to coerce you from flowing in a direction of your higher self or a route of positivity, it is often how you are drawn in, that obstructs the flow. It is at this moment to really be in self-awareness to be in control and almost to take charge and be assertive in your actions. Often any decisions made from a place of stress or fear would present a different outcome to your perceived outcome. Life is always in a continuous cycle whether it be a vicious or a balanced one. Again, it is your sole responsibility for the choices you make that implicates the actions you take that predicts the outcome.

Ego: the subjective of oneself to the lower vibrational frequency. One has to surpass the tread of each footprint to overcome a challenge, learn a lesson through an experience. However, one cannot get through without the other. There is a duality and opposites in all aspects of existence. You cannot perceive light unless you have gone through darkness to overcome the hurdles, challenges are a testament to one's evolution. You need to experience opposites and equals in and within the elements too.

We have daylight, the sun rises, we have the night and the moon, there is hot - heat summer, cold-winter. Black-White; yin yang, the masculine-feminine...male-female so undeniably there is our higher self and lower self the ego...

Take a moment to learn the energy space you are in that stance and pause and breathe before taking any decisions, stand firm in making that decision and weighing up emotional feelings from where you are in that space, is it a positive place or negative place? We are humans with a mass of energy. It is this very energy that is connected to the Universe creating a universal wavelength through frequency and vibrations. What you put out will attract, your thought process needs to match the vibration and frequency of your choice to present you with the desired outcome. Each aspect of your being, mind, body and spirit has a language that resonates to the tones and rhythm of the universe, your vessel, the physical body speaks through body language, the mind talks- it simply just chatters and the physical obeys. Your journey of life can be infinite and wholesome, encased in love, for when you arise from any restrictions and above any limitations you are fully liberated. The language of the Universe is LOVE. This is THE ultimate powerhouse and the connection. Love is an existence, the wholeness and creation of all that you are in true essence of your soul. Love is to be in love with life, your life is a gift, the soul within you is the gem, a treasure, a precious mass of energy, your being, that resides within you, without this you are just a shell, a carcass, you are not living just dead simple as that. Your worthiness is a lot more than you give yourself credit for? Beautiful soul you are created in the likeness of the very creator that put you on earth, the contract you took for this mission and purpose, to live, learn and experience those contracted lessons. Your soul knows but you are yet far from understanding any value. Love is the epitome of all that you are, from the presence and beyond, you are love beyond measure, Love is the fuel of your soul that connects you through to source, to the universe, to God.

Do you recognise who you are? Can you answer by asking yourself WHO AM I? When you truly connect within and recognise who you truly are, your purpose here is defined. You are a powerful being of creation, the exterior is only a vessel, within you is the most sacred jewel...your SOUL...there is no higher purpose than recognising the divine that is within. No matter what is going on, make every second, minute, hour, day, month, year count. My mantra: I am love; I am light; I am all that I am; within me is my inner sanctuary, where I find the resonance of all that is. Why question when the answers lie within. My light is my flame of divinity fuelled by all the love that I am

For the beautiful soul that you are, allow not the shadows of darkness to dim your path. The flame of divinity within, is the light that fuels the love always. Where there is consistent light there is always eternal divine love, this power lights the flame within to shine brightly to eternity and beyond. We are one consciousness, we are all in oneness, flow in this love, fear not, just allow the lessons to unfold and experience ahead, know all is as it should be, raise not the fear but the expectation of a fulfilling journey of oneness and connection. You, me and all are oneness, nothing sets us apart, one consciousness is all, the only indifference is the mechanics, data, genetics of one's being. Your soul is the divine aspect of Love that is within you always. When you deviate from this, the energy dynamics change the wavelength of the flow of the journey, the masterpiece of one's destination.

I AM

I AM that I AM in the presence of all that is, in this powerful magnitude of Universal flow, totally interconnected to true source of one consciousness. I AM this glorious joy, an infinite being in the impossibility of all possibility... Recognise the creation you are, your purpose here is to complete the mission of your soul. You are an incredible worthy human being; nothing else matters but who you are, give to yourself this honour for the masterpiece that you are, glorify in the infinity of LOVE, for this is the divine within you, the purpose of all that you are, unfolds perfectly by understanding who you truly are? A beautiful soul. Honour thyself, honour others as they cross your path, for we are all ONE journeying through this mighty Planet Earth...Thank you Mother Earth as we thread our footprints, Thank you Father heaven, for our creation! I AM all that I AM, a beautiful being in this oasis of vastness and oneness.

Step into your own presence to become aware and take control. Everything and anything can become a blame game, this happened, that happened, and so forth. Are you not taking reins to control your own life, you alone are responsible for controlling yourself and not allowing yourself to be controlled? There is a huge difference being in control and being controlled, for each will serve a different outcome. It is none of my business what anyone else does, what I do is my concern for this will predict the outcome of any circumstances you find yourself in. Achieving is victory, failing to achieve is the downfall, you were not in control of the execution of your desired plan and purpose. Did you set a plan, did you have a purpose? or were you in denial, and just had an assumption or expectation of the outcome, which ends up not being your desired outcome. Disappointment can only arise, if your desired intentions were not the outcome. There has to be an implementation of a method to a plan to succeed. If the outcome is failure, then ask yourself did you plan to fail or failed to plan. I always use the latter as a mantra **'plan to fail- failed to plan'**.

Life always offers mysterious answers for whatever is meant to be for this is always in Source/Universe/God's plan. Your ideas and your dreams are yours, they are put in your head by source as an inspiration to follow them, for its divine's way to implant for the perfect plan. It is your choice and free will to act upon them as intuition. Wisdom and guidance are not a mere coincidence, messages or communication may flow in many ways but it is the action taken to materialise them. Anything that is planted will flourish to fruition if you nurture it in the first instance to reach the desired intended goal.

Our brain is the power box in our head. The most powerful organ in the human body, it controls the body, your physical, through signals to which the body responds and vice versa. The brain is the seat of intelligence, the interpreter of the senses, initiator of body movements and controller of behaviour. The brain is the source of all the qualities that define our humanity. It houses our mind the subconscious and conscious matter. The mind is the manifestations of thought, perception, emotion, determination, memory and imagination that takes place within the brain.

Your subconscious mind is a powerful force to be reckoned with. It makes up around 95% of your brain power. Mind power is one of the strongest and most useful powers you possess. This power, together with your imagination, can create success or failure, happiness or unhappiness, opportunities or obstacles. ... Mind power is composed of your attention, your mental images and your thoughts.

Kim Dhaliwal

Think of a puppet show. A marionette controls a puppet through wires and signals, to put on a desired effect. Its carrying out its function to the desired presentation of the show.

Failure does not have to be defeat, but a learning curve of what does not work and another attempt to make it right.

We are all part of this amazing earth planet, and exist in the world within it. The corridors of living are not to exist in any darkness that may prevail, but to open one's eyes to the potential of the light that shines from within, yet one cannot always perceive it. Attempt to take stance in your power, because within this almighty presence of YOU radiates a powerful divine light. This is your support system that is often overlooked or neglected, you are always fully supported from your precious soul that exists within the vessel of you. This soul of yours shines and infuses you with unconditional love, yet your humanness suppresses it. Don't let the darkness in to take over and invade your being, for this is what feeds the lower ego. Allow the power of the divine light ease the burdens of heaviness. Don't carry the cloak of darkness, instead wear the robe of eternal light, shine it with love. The divinity exists within you, light the flame don't douse it. You will be amazed at the transformation that alights from the vessel. Painful lessons and experiences pave a way forward to a change, which is often resisted!

Resistance is persistence, and being in your comfort zone can become habitual, it takes courage to step out. For years I have been very comfortable retreating to my peaceful sanctuary "MY HOME" not my temple, my actual dwellings. The ambience of being in place in peace amongst my personal haven. As my daughter always puts it 'I am a social recluse' yes, I guess I was to a point and still am. However, I did enjoy going out and meeting and socialising with friends, then retreated back home, had holidays with my daughter, and never away from home, more than was necessary. So, when I was offered a cabin retreat with likeminded souls, I got curious and excited at the same time. Soon as I booked and paid for the 3.5day cabin retreat, I felt apprehension building up...nervous anxiety at what I had done. There was no going back now, the payment was non-refundable, plus I was going to be with friends and not strangers. Finally, I came round to acceptance and when the day arrived to go, I had a surprising unfoldment. The journey to the destination was smooth, scenic and full of signs and synchronicities for this perfect retreat to uplift, revitalise and rejuvenate me. Needless to say, WOW! When I got to the cabin, I loved it! The 3.5days of pure magic of big lessons and soul searching as well as fun. It changed my perception. Therefore, always strive for the unexpected to gain a surprise element that exceeds your expectations.

Throughout our journey of life, collectively so many beings resist change so much. Changes are an awakening to new beginnings and awareness.... purification of the soul, letting go, elimination of what was and is of no more. Embracing the power of you, your divine wholesome blueprint of all that you were, the precious soul before your incarnation on planet earth. Embrace, soak, nurture, self-love. Bask the glorious super light from within all its purity, to activate all that was already there to its natural wholesome pureness, that got lost and indented through programs of life school by human directives.

It is through your challenges you rise, through your weakest you become your strongest. Embrace and fight your way through, life is what you make of it! Not what life makes it for you.

One morning I got up, and quickly jotted down a message I had just received, I felt the enormity of this message as it channelled through me, it was very meaningful for not only me, but also to resonate with you the reader. Take what you feel this message is giving you too.

"*For the beautiful soul that you are, let the light always shine, where there is consistent light, there is also always eternal divine love, this power lights the flame within you to shine brightly to eternity and beyond. I am very much you, as you are of me…one consciousness…we are all in oneness, share this love, fear not, just allow the lessons to unfold to this experience, flow forward into it, and feel that all is as it should be, raise not the fear but the expectation of a fulfilling moment, into an experience of your present journey…oneness. You are me, and I am you… nothing sets us apart…one consciousness is all, the divine is within you always, distance is only created when you look elsewhere.*

The light shines upon all those that request it, it is never far out of reach, we are constantly within as we support your journey of enlightenment, your soul is your connection, so you are never far from these realms, you already are very much part of the light, yet it is the daily harbours of life existence on earthly planes that cloud your judgement which shrouds your perception of being.

Where there is light there is love, where there is that ebb of darkness there is always hope".

From that speck of hope, find your 'I am that I am', and who you choose to be, after all, the 'I am' is just an exploration to get to the real you. You may have taken the steps and walked the path, with the choices and decisions to get to your destination, yet if still question the failures, then what have you really learned and not understood. You are who you are not, by choice or decision but of your own making, yet you easily question the failure, and forget to be appreciative of any minuscule or major successes. There is no reason to search, to look and to blame when, what is apparent is to overcome any block by just continuing to reach the intention, by just attempting continuously to reach it, until it automatically flows towards you. It is a lack of self-perseverance, when you just attempt to reach and then give up at the first hurdle which becomes a deflated effort of failure.

PRACTICE

I AM, in total connection in the ebb and flow of life, everything in life is how you react to it. Give it some thought, positive actions will manifest a positive outcome, time is a skill,

Allow not the thought to control, but to mastermind your thought,

Practice makes perfect, practice becomes an art, not a task

Succumb to weakness and it overwhelms, overcome with strength and you have succeeded. Practice is the tool to gear your purposes in the right direction

So it is, and so mote it be!

Mother Teresa Quote:

Be faithful in small things, because it is in them that your strength lies

Chapter 5

WILL

If one was to see and be aware of what is beyond this veil (the spiritual plane of existence) to that of (Earth's plane of existence) they would not have the desire to push towards their trajectory but instead have the expectation that it's all there, it doesn't work like that. There must be an input of desire to meet or reach a set point, similar to a visualisation that will manifest only through efforts not just for it to materialise. One has to have the will, and drive to input to receive output. I asked my spirit team to elaborate "If we can see, hear your visions, and this is a part of the planned destiny, of the chosen lessons to be learned and taught to one self as a crucial growth experience it will be orchestrated to the directive of that vision. The belief of one self should be that it will be able to learn from others in a meaningful manner that is beneficial for them. The strength that you feed into the vision is the ability of your mind. To navigate your thoughts through your body is the power you possess and you can see the results that will be reflected through your efforts"

Nothing is impossible without your presence of commitment to yourself, and your ability to make progress through your actions, and your ability of being successful with the process that you have chosen for yourself to succeed in, and with your ability of doing than not doing. The seed is the thought from an idea you have created and the opportunity that you have, will come to fruition as you grow and develop your skills in the process of making the seed more effective for the purpose. It has been planted for a reason, if you chose to tend to it by nurturing the roots of your seed it will grow from the input of the strength and love you give to it. If you choose to have a momentary harvest then the seeds will wilt and excitement will be gone too. The mind is an intellectual system that drives the body to action, but it will also select what it feels and the body will readily adjust to that because of a previous pattern and programme. The power is to be in awareness of this and override the system to decode to deconstruct the programme in the (mind) drive to operate from a new direction, that has not happened before. Perseverance is required and it is at this point the fault can become a failure. The mind consistently needs a MOT to operate. The MOT you give to it will be how that part works efficiently and effectively. You wouldn't drive a car consistently without rectifying a fault because it will not pass. It will be deemed as failed. This is what you need for your mind. The operation system needs to follow a new manual, for effective resulting performance.

I am the Will, for through this it is thy Will to become what Will be, it is within the presence of me that becomes the recognition of what is. I have the power to drive forth this vessel to achieve whatever my Will is.

My Will today is to focus, my aim is to listen, through this I Will act forth which Will be the outcome of the choices I make.

I have the Will to win, I have the Will to give up, but ultimately it is my Will that is fed by the strength I give to it. I have a choice! Do I Survive or do I fail? The greatest gift I give to me is the strength of my Will!

W-Welcome
I- I (Infinite)
L-love
L-life

Your arrival on the earth planes is welcomed when you are birthed, with such infinite love, of a precious life. This is the gift of you, so don't **Waste It Love Life = WILL,** ensure the trajectory of your life on departure back home goes with a grand tapestry, therefore **Weave In Lasting Legacy = WILL**

"Through the will that I am, love is the divine key to oneness"
©KDhaliwal

It is that you become of what you make of oneself, it is not the making of oneself to mould to the structures of adherence in society, but far of which is within that needs to blossom and bloom to the unfoldment of a life that is you, for a purpose to live freely that you have come for. Become that which you are, within to be who you are for such purposes for the mission that you are here to serve. Lessons and experiences are the unfoldment of that bloom, the blossoming of one's self is attained in that process of one's evolvement.

See, soak nurture and value Nature, it is forever evolving, encapsulate the wonders that endow each season, the perspective of such wonder is not just something that comes and goes. One is shown the survival, the omniscient presence is there, not just to experience and move through. Oneself becomes impatient and is wasting one's energy impatiently desiring for what is next? Next can only be perceived if you are leading and living from the presence.

Nature and the elements are teaching us, yet the majority are asleep or awakened in a stupor oblivious of what one is shown! The cycle of nature is constantly going through birth, death and rebirth. The elements of nature earth, wind, fire, air, water, metal and wood are the process through the seasons of heat, cold, wet, dry, windy, still, foggy, bright. The seasons of Winter, Spring, Summer and Autumn are also showing us, one lives in joyful experience of Summer & Autumn, some will enjoy Spring too as part of this essence, but all will be procrastinating when endowed with Winter...one does not perceive the experience of what Winter is showing, just the displeasure of experiencing what one deems the 'winter blues'. Everything within everything is a speculative wonder showing oneself the process is ever continuing to each phase/cycle and will do so. Yet does one learn the exact cycle of one's life? That is where one has to become, to be, to know, and to be who, and what purpose they are here for. Immerse within the depth of who you are in this vast planet, and through that knowing you become to know and experience that very existence of you!

Winter: Time of hibernation, darker nights. One goes within but does one really? This season ends in part of latter year and continues into the next new year. What does this show us, what are we learning? Other than mass majority complaining of the cold, dark nights, snow, frost, dipping of temperatures and so on. One needs to open their eyes and view what winter is showing, learn from the animal kingdom if one cannot get or fathom an understanding. Everything within everything is showing us, but is one learning?

Spring: Rebirth. Nature is awakening, the bulbs in the ground and seedlings are spurting forth to blossom and flourish. The leaves on the branches of each tree are coming through, the animal kingdom too is showing birth.

Summer: Joy and exuberance, warmer weather and longer days, spiritual growth and progress for goals.

Autumn: Symbolic of abundance, harvest, shorter days and darker nights. Having balance and equilibrium, a transition of what has been and what will be, embracing change and letting go and being in gratitude.

Letting Go:

There is an equilibrium in everything including in life. This is the balance of all matter, what comes has to go, you receive, you also have to let go. There cannot be an up without a down, an in without an out. Nothing is guaranteed but amongst it is, all and much more.

What is now will become too late in the future, bitterness, feuds, arguments are all man-made or created. It severs the vital purpose of a life of living. If love is the embodiment of life, why is there a need to create havoc, this turmoil is not an experience of pleasure but hatred and war from oneself and within. So much is lost when there is so much to gain. Regrets are too late and to live a burden of them going forward, you suppress the very life out of you. Every choice has an outcome, and every outcome has that very cause and effect of unfoldment to that choice. The delivery of that outcome is that decision that one made.

To simplify if we celebrate a birth, why do we commiserate a death. Birth is a life to live, love, learn and experience, this is the fullness and ecstasy of life in total equilibrium and embodiment. If life is fulfilled to these criteria, it has completed a mission of its intention and purpose of that contract of life. Therefore, this completion too should be a celebration too!

Some will lack in understanding how does a young life gone too soon be celebrated, when an opportunity has not been there to live fully. This depth of insight is not to be understood by all if any, yet those that do will be the enlightened ones in the acceptance of what life and living is. As I mentioned previously, there is a cycle in everything, a beginning and an ending, a start to a completion.

Please I ask my soul and higher guides to answer this complexity that is so misunderstood yet needs to have an understanding to accept the balance.

View it as an overcharge on a price, you would debate the difference and attain the refund to offset the balance of the difference. Same as the principle if you were late for work you would make the time up to balance the difference.

Therefore if a soul contract of a life has not been fulfilled to the expiration length, and has deceased too soon, for example a soul contract is to be fulfilled to the age of 70 years, yet life suddenly or unexpectedly expires at the age of 50years, there will be a shortfall of 20years. Therefore, these lessons in life school of humanity remain unfulfilled, and not experienced as per the mission of the soul contract that they took. This is that soul that has to rebirth, to the life expectancy of 20 years of age, for completion of the lessons outstanding from the previous cycle of life. Life is to be appreciated no matter what, why, how and when. The wonder is the joyous of what is in the presence. Often enough the rawness of sadness, heartache, robs one from looking deeper into the gratitude and blessings of what that life taught and left one with. Appreciate time because it serves a lot! Time is lost so much in transition for useless waste less energy expended into what is not meaningful, that so often becomes the most important things that have been missed on one's trajectory of life. Make the importance of time, life and moments count now, not when it's a little too late.

Miscarriages, still birth and infant deaths need to be understood, but often enough the commiseration that follows takes hold of ones living into turmoil of the loss. A soul will choose its parents, but it will always have a choice to leave too, if it finds that the energies do not correlate or resonate to them, it will make a choice to depart. If we look at the role of the parents that have to endure the loss and parting, they do have a sense of knowing but the grief would overwhelm the acceptance and understanding of that.

Again timing comes to play in every essence of all. Timing was offset on this occasion but it doesn't mean that the time will be presented again for this, all at the right timing, one needs to accept, let go, be and allow what needs to come. All in divine timing in equilibrium and perfect balance and order. This is the ratio and cycle of all that begins has to end, that which remains incomplete too, needs completion. How this happens is not for us to dwell on and understand, but to be in acceptance of what is here in the now, because this very moment we are breathing, we are living, we have control. You understand this then you will have understood your gratifying existence of you. Recognise you, yourself, your being is your worth. Live, breathe, love who you are, nothing else matters. Just get to know you and that itself is the most powerful part of your existence....YOU. Honour you in the highest ranking beyond everything, and within that you will be in alignment of all that needs to flow in perfect harmony in recognition of whom you are? You get you, and all else just flows!

Challenges are there to make you a stronger version of you, to overcome and not be defeated. You can only become the best version of yourself to achieve the accolade of the highest ranking through such experiences, it's a part of life. You always have that choice you either flow to overcome, or be defeated to be suppressed. Your choice? It is this choice that delivers the desired effect.

To give you an example of my own experience relating to my health. I lost the will, the hope, and the flow of my weight~ over the last few years there were no excuses as I had so much on with the fullness of caring duties towards both my parents, yet I was always more conscious of my weight and wellbeing. I always attempted, at least I tried, and yeah there was some weight loss in a yo yo extent, what came off went back on, yet I was aware, and at that point controlled it from not going over a certain point. Despite last year being the toughest, I still managed to maintain a routine of exercising either walking or yoga, and sometimes both! Deep down I was aware in my mindset, that my weight was contributed to stress and a poor lifestyle of eating. The stress I was under, would not help towards reaching any goal, due to my system being flushed with cortisol, which would hold onto the weight. I took it in my stride, that any effort of attempt would not yield any results to the desired affects. Yet my attempts at least gave the yo yo weight loss and weight on effect, it was something of a slight effort of input than of nothing, so I convinced myself!

However, this year 2023, I concluded after doing my dearest mum's ashes. I would return to my life that once was. I agree 6 years is a long time overdue to make up. I cannot account for these years as a living, but I was most certainly going through the toughest challenges, and they were a part of my lessons as an evolvement of my human growth. These 6 years taught me a lot! This isn't about the past anymore, it's about the NOW... I am ashamed to say, that I have been out of control with my eating, it's crazy and I am absolutely aware of what I am putting in my mouth. The worst of it is, I just can't be bothered to do any form of exercise now. It's pure laziness. I've never been like this. I have gained further weight, tipped over the scales I never allowed myself to get beyond, yet I still am not doing anything. My back pain is always the first sign to let me know my body can't cope carrying the additional weight, it's burdensome. In the past I always acknowledged this and did something about it! Always with amazing success. What is going on I ask. I have no excuses. I have all the time to exercise, prepare and plan too....WHAT IS GOING ON I ask my soul/ higher self to reveal?

This is a challenge on your human level. It's not about a spiritual evolution. What you have to overcome is the ability to create a mindset of being happy, accepting something that you can apply a change with a positive attitude and desire. This is only down to you, the saboteurs of thyself is you, no one is forcing you. You have responsibility for yourself. If we ask the actions you overtake on thyself, do you feel they are good choices. Are you in awareness of the consequences of those choices. You are oblivious, yet you complain. You feel unhappy. Your thoughts create the emotions and feelings. Therefore, if you subject yourself in full responsibility of awareness of what you are doing, then those consequences will be to that effect.

You are not happy with yourself, you have already answered that, but what actions are you taking to change that disposition. You complain about your weight, yet instead of applying a positive attitude, you continue with a negative attitude. Your body is speaking to you, are you tuning in. This intelligent system is crying out for help for perfect balance and equilibrium.

You are aware, yet ignorance is your bliss in this present stance. The choices you make are down to you. If you are not happy, change what is not working. The strength of your WILL to overcome and defeat, is the power that will drive it. We are always here to support you, but importantly the lack of support you honour your needs are diminished.

Your body is signalling through your laboured breathing, your movement is lethargic, your energy levels have a great input, however upon exertion you suffer, your back is crying out, it can't support the additional baggage you carry. Your head space - foggy brain, confidence, avoidance of social events- it's all there. Sugar rush is temporary allowing a high dopamine level "feel good factor" it's not sustainable and doesn't last. This destructive cycle is just that, it continues on. Take an inventory of thyself to understand the importance of the emotional eating you are subjecting yourself for comfort. You cannot preach, teach, advocate something if you are not prepared to do the same for yourself. We cannot tell you what to do, you already have the answers. Contingent upon to change your present stance towards a solution towards oneself to obtain your desired result and outcome for that happiness. "Thank you" for this insight my beloved team, higher self and soul.

The dawning for me is, I'm taking refuge in overwhelming indulgence of an emotional pattern through comfort eating.

The loss of both my parents, has left a void, that I'm trying to compensate with food. I am aware these temporary food fixes will not fill that void. I am also aware, what my parents would be thinking now of what I'm subjecting myself too. I am ashamed. I am better than this. I know I can do this. I have to do it for myself. I owe it to me. I am going to take control especially of my naughty brain. It seems to think it knows what my body needs, will consistently offer the temptations for me to succumb to. The battle has come to defeat the brainwashing. I need to tame the brain matter of temporary dopamine hits, which can be obtained another positive way. The challenge is to overcome these old habits and patterns to make way for new ones. Here commences the journey.

Today it starts, not tomorrow, not next week. There is no time like the present. It is just that, it's time now!

As I just finished writing this, I had the word "all in moderation" come through. I know what this means. Eat what is necessary, not overload or under load, for me it's the former. I don't stop at one piece of chocolate, I eat the whole bar, 1 biscuit, it's a packet of biscuits, crisps, sweets, ice cream etc etc. so it goes on….

What is my will, will be thy will- control the mind that coheres the body through emotions, and feelings that causes you to act from those feelings. Divert and take ownership to manipulate the mind what it is exactly that is needed, to achieve the intention you set. It does not happen without you defeating what is presented, the power is to overcome such obstacles to get the effective desire of your intention/s. Nothing can be achieved without attempting to overcome to get to the desired goal, yet everything is all within reach. You are far far superior than you think, yet you are lost. Find your way through the circuits and input the desired imprint to navigate your way through. The mechanism is there for you to access.

I can and I will do this, I am in control of my mind and not my mind over my body and emotions.

My own perfect example as above, in this scenario was to find my way: Over the last few years through grief, caring role and covid I gained weight, I blamed stress and cortisol - a primary stress hormone. For the past few years, I continuously set the same intention to achieve my weight loss, claiming this is it! and yet my attempts only succeeded part way, all too soon given up to get back to where I started, (recall the yo yo effect). I was just not in the right circumstances, to allow my mindset to adhere, and follow accordingly, specifically as there was so much going on in my personal life.

If some things are started then they must be concluded to the desired effect of that goal, that then becomes within reach far beyond any expectation you put forth upon oneself. Almost too easily, the mind tricks the body through the emotions by subjecting you to succumb to those feelings that are evoked, and I guess the uninvited house guest in my system- the stress hormone, was not only invading, and overtaking control, but mostly a hindrance to any desired progress. Would anyone in their right mind unintentionally warrant an uninvited stranger into their living abode, to cause or wreak havoc in their present equilibrium. I don't think so! Imagine the consequences of unbalance and disarray. My lesson through this was ingrained, and taught, and still continues to teach through this integral health journey.

This was the same intention of the book that needed to be written, yet in those 6 years there was not an in depth of material to substantiate the wisdom attained. The perfect plan and time was now. Excuses are a part of human nature; these are the emotions most will readily give in to. Bring your focus and attention to what it is that you seek, are you on track, what obstacles are presented. List your emotion, understand your feeling, don't suppress it, acknowledge it, and overcome it by navigating oneself, one can either pause, reflect and move on, or give in to the entrapment of what the mind thinks you need, which may prompt you to readily given in to that in agreement. Life will present such hurdles and obstacles, because there is a learning or an experience to be gained, and mostly unbeknown to you the timing may just not be right at that moment.

Trust and believe in YOU. What matters is just being, in the presence of all that is...finding you is the ultimate true completeness, in the wholeness of this vastness. YOU are your power, shine your light, illuminate your path, this is your journey, all that you are, and all that you become.

Today declare: *I AM, in charge of me. Each positive action and word within my life are my choices and my decisions that create my destiny. Believe this and believe the results you create!*

SYMPHONY

I AM, in tune with the rhythms of the Universe.

May the music of your soul make your spirit dance to the tunes of your life journey creating a perfect symphony.

The first note was when we all first arrived on the earth plane, the wail was not a crying but a chorus of your soul to heaven.

You my beautiful soul are the instrument of your life, once this lifetime is completed, all the melodies will have orchestrated a beautiful symphony. Melody of love is the language of this Universe, tap into this reservoir.

This symphony of love is the fulfilment of life that fuels this vessel of mine

Without love there is only a void of emptiness, this love fuels my inner temple and divinity in perfect equilibrium of life itself!

So it is, and so mote it be!

Chapter 6

UNIVERSAL SUPPORT

The year 2014 was a testing time for me. I finally took the courage to leave a secure fulltime senior position in a corporate firm. I fought with my higher self, the if's and but's. Yet on the same token I was not happy doing what gave me security and an income. I was ferociously battling a Jekyll and Hyde persona, but I needed to free my spirit from the suppression of what may be deemed as a norm. It is a programming that we have to work to earn a living and so forth, but to the detriment of not fulfilling a joyful and happy existence. I knew from my soul aspect I was not serving my purpose, yet still fearful how was I going to live, thrive, survive and continue.

Alongside working full time, I had built a reputable holistic business in all my spare time, evenings and weekends. It did not guarantee the high income I was accustomed to receiving each month from a full-time job. However, I had a work life balance and was totally passionate about being of service to those that needed it. I subjected myself to the fears that did arise, however listened to my heart and never regretted my decision.

It was quite a testing time for me specifically, so I left in the start of summer. In hindsight I didn't think. It was a quiet period for a holistic business. Children off school, and it was family vacation time. The prospect of not earning for the next six weeks felt hugely fearful. It felt strange to suddenly experience these negative dips. I did not like them as normally I always was in positive spirits, and yet here I was doubting whether the Universe was supporting me, I was also questioning where my Angels were? I had called out on several occasions; desperate energy had stepped in. I simply was not in tune and letting go to just trust.

I knew the low dip that I was suddenly experiencing, was from the prospect of not having a guaranteed income for all my outgoings. In full time employment there was this safety net, yet hand on heart irrespective of how I was feeling I knew I had made the right decision to leave my full-time secure job, this huge leap of faith was indeed the RIGHT decision, and there certainly was no doubt over this, yet here I was now feeling a nagging churning within me where and how were the finances going to come at the end of the month to pay the mortgage and bills etc. I felt I was not getting any support from the Universe or my beloved Angels, how wrong was I!

This was the human part of me reacting and being impatient. Time seems crucial to us on the earth planes, yet in the ethereal planes time does not exist, time is existing in the omnipresent. Obviously, the Universe and my beloved Angels had heard my pleas and requests, they were busy orchestrating behind the scenes.

In order to achieve an income, my second huge letting go release was pending. I had worked so hard achieving one of many goals, of owning a luxury dream car, it was my pride and joy. Yet in my current circumstance I did not need a luxury vehicle, and it meant to let go to downsize to something smaller and economical. Miraculously when it did happen, it was so spontaneous that I did not have chance to think or react. I felt euphoric and a sense of relief, the whole process itself felt quite magical.

Strangely when I retract back to the beginning of the week of that summer, the magic was already transpiring behind the scenes. I was calling out to the Universe for financial assistance and requesting to my beloved Angels to send me the perfect buyer for my car.

Well by the end of the week the Universe and the Angels not only found me the perfect buyer for my car, but also the additional finances to support me to pay all my outgoings and a little extra for the next few months.

Later that night, I looked at the empty parking spot outside of my window, and felt a little pang but allowed that to come up and pass. I reassured myself that my car had given me the best three years memories of driving, and the care I had also given it. I did manage to sleep well, but awoke at 4am and my thoughts drifted to my beautiful car. Why was I feeling like this over a piece of metal, and here I am writing I guess just to settle my feelings of letting go.

When I look back to my week, strange synchronicities were already occurring. On Thursday morning I washed and cleaned my car even though it did not need doing. Normally I always took it to a local place where the guys always jet washed and cleaned my car and this was only done a week ago. I guess my higher self knew, and was preparing me, this was my goodbye and thanks to my car for all that it had provided me. I then received a call from the dealership offering me a brand-new car at super discounts on a part exchange deal, I arranged a time to go and see them on Friday, but this did not happen, as other events took place, therefore I had to cancel and re- arrange for Monday. This too was not going to happen as my car was sold on Sunday, to someone who approached me, and offered me a cash deal that was beyond my expectation, yet totally deserving of it!

The other amazing occurrence is how the Universe has managed to put the right people in place on my path at the time I needed morale support, a further boost to lift me from my low dips. I am eternally grateful for this and those people "Thank You"

UNIVERSE

I AM, graciously living a life of gratitude "Thank you, Universe"

I receive wholly that what the Universe provides.

I connect with a positive mindset aligned equally with a positive energy in body, to attract the lavish abundance that I am deserving.

These positive thoughts are the powerlines to the Universe. "Thank you, Universe"

Each and every day I am provided, I am feeling the love in my heart as that's where my gratitude resides, I am feeling the power of my mind, as that's were my thoughts resides in perfect alignment.

I am so grateful for all the lessons, experiences, my journey.

I joyfully celebrate my evolvement of my entire being of who I am.

I receive with gratitude and blessings the cosmic abundance of all gifts that are my birth right, I am loving life! I AM in the presence of all that is, and more in this mighty universal flow…and so it is for ALL.

So it is, and so mote it be!

Never doubt or ignore any nudging or message was my lesson, yet further down my journey I became ignorant to another nudging that I just seemed to pass off as my mind thinking it.

In March 2015 I finally heeded a calling that I was initially getting way back at the beginning of the year in January!

I was receiving the nudging from my Guides and Angels to elicit healing through Meditation from our Divine Mother Mary, and this was to be done run up to Easter. In hindsight my higher self was preparing me to intercept this nurturing divine unconditional love. For a few months Mother Mary had been coming through…in my healing sessions as well as in my personal relaxing space. As I write this piece, she has again bestowed her presence…perhaps Easter Sunday the resurrection of Jesus Christ is physically…spiritually and emotionally apt, I am basking in divine healing as I write, I feel the effects of this will also be healing for each recipient reading this. It was a deep intense day full of love, healing and peace.

The Divine Mother Mary graced me with her presence again during a group meditation. I am eternally grateful, to you Divine beloved Mary, the Universe and our Creator. This was the perfect day for this magical healing Meditation for my group. The room was filled with so much divine love, the energy was surreal as we basked in this divine glory…I am most honoured for this experience as were my group of ladies…Thank you Universe…I am most grateful to fulfil, and be part of this service for the highest healing of all concerned, each of us have benefited a surreal and breath-taking experience so magical yet so in depth of the phenomenal energy.

To you readers, it is not words and speech you are absorbing right now, it is the powerful effect, the knowing and perhaps the sparkle of curiosity rising in you. This healing channelled message came to me, as I share with you for the most profound healing effect:

"Feel me as I feel you my child, you are the Earth Angel, reach out and touch your presence on those that you encounter, for it is not what you have planned, but what the plan of the divine that is bestowing upon you. A step that unfolds is not just a mere tread upon your path, but a unique experience of a lesson that is just in the unfolding as a part of the big plan.

Dear One feel with your heart, see through your third eye and touch from your depth of intuition. Embrace this magic, as you merge and connect and reach to the scopes of these planes, your heavenly team awaits to support and guide you in such miraculous ways, lead by example and the rest will just fall in the divine perfect way.

All is as it is; questions just raise a doubt when answers flow with such mystery. The planes evoke each transitional phase, shed what no longer serves, fulfil for all that will leave but an endearing impact.

You are the chosen one, because you choose to be, the soul, the spirit are in sync, the tolerant mind too can be stabilised to flow in this sync. Reach deep within, search this temple that has always been a part of you. Unlock the mystery to unfold the love, the light and the power of you. It is all there to access, you are the owner of the key; find it at your will, if it is your choice to choose as this is the will to unlock you to be the chosen one. After all it is only a choice, which leads to a direction, a direction that is a part of the unfolding journey that forms the decision.

Hesitations are just a mere pause, reflect momentarily…encompass and glide positively. Open and greet what awaits, divine light, showers of blessings and unconditional love and much more… this is more and more of what you can handle. Let's begin our journey my child. A simple word begins to unfold a page to an endearing journey for a breathless encapsulating story.

I grace you not only with love but surmountable peace...in the knowledge that all is as it should be, ascend to these planes to feel the joy for that not only serves you but all those that are in need of it. As I touch your heart, feel your spirit, your soul resonate with mind and body to synchronise to this heightened oneness...you are never alone"

Thank you, dearest beloved Mother Mary, for your words of grace and love.

Miracles of Angelic Intervention

The Universe exists within us, in the depths of the chambers of our hearts. That spark, that flame of divinity. It is alight and fuelled by love, a love of existence, of life, of breath of oneness. We have to awaken to our mission here, define that purpose of what we are here for. That is our pre incarnation contract, majority of who will be furthest from fulfilling their mission due to set conditions and programming of societal living.

I knew I was different from a very young tender age; my development was still ongoing; I was not aware of it at this age of 5. Along the way there were many challenges, these were part of my growth and evolvement until came the time of knowingness that all is not what is, but more, and yet unexplainable, to acknowledge and embrace it, was something totally different and alien. This was and is not a recognised norm but deemed nonsense or non-existent.

When I reflect back there were so many occurrences going on. I always felt a presence/s around me, be it guides or angels protecting me. I couldn't see or hear them but I felt them strongly. As the eldest of three, I was always isolated. I was always treated differently to my two younger brothers, I am sure both my parents loved me, I know my dad doted on me, and I had so much love and affection from him. Rather than go into depths of my childhood, I reflect on the incidences that occurred that formed me to my presence of who "I AM".

My journey may have started at the tender age of five, but perhaps I was not ready, and did not acknowledge anything until my teenage years aged 16. My insight to certain experiences made me aware but yet fearful, and so much in denial that I did not either want to understand, let alone accept what was unfolding. I felt frightened to lack of understanding or acknowledging what a profound gift I was bestowed with. Therefore, I kept ignoring it.

As well as sensing, I was also seeing visions. I always felt a mighty presence over or around me. Anything I saw i.e., premonition, came true the following next few days/weeks. It was a surreal unexplainable experience growing up. If I said anything I was made fun of and ridiculed. To the point I just shut up, and closed inwards, I just felt I was the odd one out. Something was wrong with me, even to the point where my parents got a priest involved to ward off what should not be there, and instead bless me… didn't help…because no one understood!

It was not until my twenties I went through a massive cathartic experience, an episode in my life that would be a catapult to open my awareness into the light and beyond. My peace, my solace and comfort came from this source.

My spiritual awakening is indeed an endearing journey and continues to be. Experience has nothing to do with making you an individual better than another; every moment in each day is a breath of life existence, awareness but also a memorable capturing experience. It's the captivating magical moments that create the person that you are "I am no better than you, as you are of me" We are all unique in our individual ways, each of us giving, learning and evolving. After all this is what our journey is all about; lessons to evolve to who we are today, and we will be going forward.

My divine path gave me the enlightenment, the courage, the strength and much more. Angels are a very big part of my life, my creator sent the mercy of his Angels to support me, and I am forever indebted, eternally grateful for each and every day.

As I progressed further into my spiritual awareness, I still felt unsettled as if there was still an element missing, nothing seemed quite fulfilling although I felt as though my lessons in my personal journey were completed, there was still something more. An impatient yearning that not all was yet complete, there was still a missing fraction to make it whole, even though I was a fully qualified Holistic Practitioner there was still a piece missing out of the puzzle. I had an urgent desire within me, that what I had thought was completed was in fact still very much uncompleted. Deep within me, my intuition was nudged by my beloved Angels, the answer was there, yet I was oblivious to it. My head was shouting reiki, yet my heart and my whole being knew it was not just reiki itself. The healing doors were opening and the essence of Angels is where the answer lay, right there from the start. Where and who I am today has been from the pure love essence of the Angelic realms via our creator. This team supported my needs through healing, comfort and an opening to an amazing enlightenment.

This is what I wanted to bring through, the joy, the love, the peace and the Angels performing the healing through me. It was the Angels that pushed me to seek further; this is when my blinkers finally fell off, the answer staring right in front of my eyes. It was Angelic Reiki, a most beautiful beyond words experience. Tears rolled down my eyes, this was the start to another miraculous part of my journey and still continues to be to this day, above all a very humbling and unique experience.

It is such an honour that your body becomes a doorway to the higher planes of the Angelic realms, where they all await in line, to step in to heal the recipient, who's soul has called out for that healing. I am so humbled to have been a part of this process as I have witnessed how I have touched many lives through this magical healing modality, knowing that in my heart, my mind, my soul and spirit, through the Angels I have made a difference, even to those that were sceptical have had an altered opinion.

I have been endowed with so many profound experiences from a real visitation from an angel through meditation, and once when I was walking home in treacherous wintery conditions.

Both experiences were full of so much unconditional love. It is a powerful love that you just want it to continue and continue, and as it fades you are left with a joyous exuberant feeling of happiness, love, purity and contentment. But when it starts to fade your whole being is shouting 'don't go'. I still smile to this day. The angel I saw was a very magical experience, it was a winter where there were so many snow and ice storms and, in the UK, this weather was declared as 'the beast from the east!'

I didn't want to drive to the local grocery store due to these conditions, I was reluctant to walk, as I had pulled my back the week before, therefore I was afraid of falling and injuring myself further. However, I managed to pluck up the courage to go extremely slowly, a 10minute journey taking me an hour. It was on the way back it became tricky. More ice was setting another layer on top of the ice already on the thick snow. I kept slipping and just praying I could get home in one piece! I was getting tired, and extremely frightened, I just wanted to be home. I happened to glance over my shoulder to see if anyone else was walking that could help me. As I looked across the street, and there I saw a most beautiful elderly female, dressed in a lovely wool coat, I noticed her soft snowy white, fluffy bouncy hair, the most gorgeous smile with red lipstick, and the gentle brightest smiling ocean blue eyes. She was absolutely glowing, and I thought to myself why is this lovely elderly lady outside in these treacherous conditions, I turned back round to see if I could help, and she was nowhere to be seen. It was just a fraction of a second, there was no explanation how she could have disappeared so fast. All I knew was, I smiled all the way home, forgot my woes and fears of falling, and was magically by my front door in less time than expected. All throughout the evening I kept questioning what on earth was this elderly lady doing outside in this cold weather? It was only when the penny dropped, I realised it was a visitation. Her beautiful appearance was shockingly striking and mesmerising. It was an Angel in disguise. She was just beaming and radiating love.

Angelic Healing:

Angelic Reiki is so profound that it not only touches and heals human life, but miraculously can be implemented to heal the environment or dwellings of the inhabitants. I recall attending a residence that required healing, from the toxicity imbedded in the environment of those living there, below is one such experience:

I was called in to heal a family who had an intense fiery situation going on amongst themselves. It became obvious as I entered the inhabitants' dwellings that it was actually their residence that was in need of vital healing, there was an intense smog and atmosphere in their house. This family had a feud going on amongst themselves to the point the anger and the arguments escalated, where by either member would ultimately bear the consequences of near to killing themselves. The parents were the main issue, but somehow the two grown children had become embroiled into the whole web of destruction, the youngest child followed whatever choices the two elder siblings made.

When I approached the family's residence, I sensed the turbulence and the intense ugly smouldering energy. The intention was to mediate between the family and heal, but unknown to me the Angels had orchestrated a different plan. The dominate male opened the door and clarified that his wife and children had gone out, he apologised that I had a wasted journey, never the less he felt inclined to talk and I felt drawn to listen and be impartial.

At the time his elderly frail mother was visiting, and she being the innocent victim had become embroiled in the whole feud. She was extremely upset and emotional. I decided she would benefit from some Angelic Reiki healing. It was during her healing treatment Archangel Michael came to me and channelled to me; healing needed to be done throughout the whole house. He motioned that I needed to infuse unconditional love and light into every corner and space of the whole house to uplift and dissipate the negative energy. He and his team as well as additional angels were standing by to support me whilst conducting this healing. All very unusual to me as I had never done anything like this, yet there was an enormous energy of support encouraging me to step up to it. I asked the permission of Mr Daw the owner of the home, who was more than accommodating to the request.

This was no ordinary house as I set forth on the task with Archangel Michael and his legion of many angels. Between us we showered 27 rooms with light and unconditional love and Angelic Reiki healing, uplifting negativity and negative energy into the light. As each room was cleansed and healed, additional angels were called in to protect each corner and window. There was a magnitude of shifting going on throughout this process.

It was not until the next day I had two revelations. Mr Daw had never apologised to anyone irrespective of whether he is in the wrong. He carries a lot of arrogance, stubbornness and authority around his being. However, the next day he approached both his elder children and apologised to them with sincerity. Mrs Daw also seemed to have mellowed down from her attitude of always being right.

Some magic was definitely taking place. The intervention of taking Angelic Reiki healing into the inhabitants living space proved to me that it is not always necessary the individuals that need to be healed, but circumstances permitting the space they are in as well.

The intensity of pressure invoked upon oneself is always self-inflicted, one needs to be in awareness that whatever situation arises, the stance is to open up to what is presented before reaction, action and aversion to the situation itself.

Sometimes in haste, the reaction can be unpredictable, which will duly cause to offset the action to be in turmoil, anger, emotional, shock or just plain dumbstruck to leave you speechless. The state of one's being should be allowed the opportunity to come into awareness of the presence.

Not every individual is the same, allow oneself to intake whatever unfolds. To give you another example:

My mother was given an "end of life" prognosis, soon after coming home from a 7-week admission in hospital. I took this news in my stride in a calm manner, knowing how much she had, and was suffering, my train of thought was for her to be released, and finally be pain free. She was now bed bound, and this was just not a life for her. My reaction was calm, the action - I just took it in my stride, that this was it, this time round it was acceptable, given the circumstances of the deterioration of mum's health. The aversion for me, as much as I didn't like it, was to only accept, as this was only a one-way ticket with no return or alternative.

However, my brother's reaction was shock, his action was not accepting and adamant there were alternatives. He was in denial and in total belief that mum was not going anywhere, and strong on intent to get the best private medical attention to make her well again. Which didn't materialise.

My dearest beloved mother, did skip through 3 end of life scenarios, there was definitely something giving her the will to survive. She wasn't ready to let go just yet, it had to be on her terms, and this was all without medical intervention. The divine was listening and giving her the time and space… more on this in chapter 8-BSD.

Another experience I would like to share was way back from 11th November 2014- It was Remembrance Day in the UK. It was such a busy day with back-to-back appointments of Angelic Healing sessions, in hindsight I didn't know what was going to unfold, other than this was a sacred day, remembering British service members who had sacrificed their lives and died in wars and other military conflicts since the onset of World War I. The place I was offering treatments was a beautiful old 14th century cottage, full of so much history itself, such a blessed and divine place.

Well, what unfolded continued very much for the rest of the day. During the session of my first client, I felt an enormous amount of energy in the room. The room was already full from the divine energies of the Angels from the angelic realm, it was more. A doorway opened from the wall at the far end of the treatment couch, and in came a surge of soldiers, lieutenants in blue greyish uniform. They just seemed to hover briefly opposite me then disappear. The presence felt almost like they had passed into the light, perhaps the angelic energies in the room and the cosmic divine light, allowed them to come through…I just couldn't comprehend at that time or explain, other than to continue on with my healing.

It did dawn on me that it was a very auspicious day, obviously Remembrance Day. This experience occurred naturally, and each of the clients treated also had such profound inexplicable healing that day. To me it was just a part of my service as normal and I thought no more of it. Normally after such a busy day of back-to-back healing sessions, I take a day out the following day to rest and recuperate my energy levels. However later that evening when I returned home, I made an concerted effort to cook a lovely meal, and was extremely grateful for the nourishment it provided me. Much to my shock the following morning instead of feeling drained and tired, I awoke in an unadulterated state of peacefulness, complete bliss from an extraordinary sleep. I just knew I was taken on an astral journey to the heavenly realms to be healed on a huge level. I just awoke in a mesmerizing beautiful state of being. I had buoyance within, and I didn't hesitate or question about going to the gym. I had an amazing run and workout, to the oblivious notion of people commenting of how much I had worked out, yet on returning home I did not feel tired! This indeed was very unusual for me, specifically from the perspective of doing full on healing treatments from the previous day, the norm usually always was Recovery Day. This didn't happen, truly I was in awe of the experience I was gifted and honoured with, and deeply grateful for it!

Experiences can come in many ways of spiritual encounters, even dreams can be special, poignant and symbolic. Never doubt or be sceptical, if you can recall a dream with as much details as possible, it maybe prophetic. Out of the many vivid dreams that I experienced, I recall one that was the most alluring, unique, loving warm experience. It was the night of the 13th going into the 14th. This was a dream, but it felt so very REAL, I just never wanted it to end, and the next day, all day it left me with a complete feeling of love, happiness and contentment. I often find myself thinking back to this dream.

In my dream I was aware I was in my bedroom; the lamps were on. The next moment I was on the street outside my house. I don't know how I got there, but there I was. The street was so quiet, it was dark other than a street lamp. I crossed over the road and faced the door of a townhouse that has 3 levels. The door was open and I walked through to a room, which seemed odd to me as I knew these types of houses do not have living quarters on ground floor. Everything felt real. I was in awe; in the middle of the room, I saw a huge bed with brown bedding with a magnificent but unusual tapestry drape. I noticed a book shelf to the right, with books on the shelves. I saw the door to the garden; the grass was so green. I was aware of a male in the room, with blond cropped hair, it was just sparkling. I could not see his face, he came towards me, I was drawn to him we embraced, this hug felt surreal, it was the most lovable and heavenly feeling, the love that I felt was so deep, a connection on a soul level. It was indescribable but felt so eternal. I just wanted it to go on and on and on, suddenly I was aware it was drawing away. I heard myself saying no, no, no please don't go. All the time I was in the experience and aware of it too, I was asleep, this did not feel like a dream, yet when the experience ended, I was aware I was back in bed. Other dreams followed, yet I was tossing and turning and yearning for the experience I had felt. The following morning, I awoke in an elated state. Throughout the day I pondered and reflected on this dream and the experience. It was so real, so good and certainly unforgettable. I tried to understand the context of this dream and the message it evoked. From my perception I assimilated:

I had received a powerful spiritual healing hug from an "Angel" during my sleep, my soul had connected at some level to receive this outpouring of love, the feeling of fulfilment. Energy needed to be exchanged during the cosmic hug, a two-way process, replenishing me as the receiver. The soul called out for it, as I may have been feeling weak, tired, and not able to continue as I was. The giver (my Angel visitation) eliminated what was not going to serve a purpose for my higher self. Beds are often seen as a symbol of symbol of privacy, peaceful times, relaxation, and retreat. Brown is an earthy colour, of humanity and humility. Bedding and tapestry- denotes an indication of one's spiritual life. It shows the way one will weave out actions in life. Its symbolic for healing and magic. Maybe I was feeling conflicted between what I wanted and what others wanted from me. To see a bookshelf suggests discipline, order, rules, and steady progress. Could possibly relate to my boundaries. Am I satisfied with the order I have established or do I continue life with decisive and strong steps to achieving mindful discipline in either material sense or spiritual sense, or both! Seeing doors related to a period of transition or change and the green grass symbolically indicate good health and success as well as a period of calm and tranquillity. I was on the cusp of a new chapter in my life that would bestow spiritual and personal peace.

Deciphering this made sense to me. I was working full time as well as building up my spiritual practice. It was time to let go of the full-time job, to pursue my path as a healer to serve mankind and humanity, to that of working in a corporate rat race negative environment.

This wonderful experience has completely fulfilled and satisfied me, as I recalled each breath-taking vivid moment. It cannot go without a token of my gratitude to my dearest Angels, angelic realms and spiritual team but above all my creator "Thank you so much!" I am extremely and eternally grateful for this beautiful heavenly experience, much needed tonic for the soul.

I could obliterate this book with so many more experiences, but I just wanted to give you the readers an insight of just a few examples.

TIME

I AM, in the presence of now, in this stance

Time is never ending, time is limitless,

in the now in this moment is everything and all.

Seconds into minutes become hours into days, that flows into weeks, to months into years.

Seasons come and go, all that changes is age, another digit to another number of your being from birth to each birth…day.

Time predicated for arrival yet the departure remains a mystery

time is a valuable commodity for being connected in the presence of each moment of one's existence…

today in this moment live life, live your existence and enjoy the moments, for tomorrow is never guaranteed to anyone.

Love life, love the passionate being that you are, for you are an embodiment of Love in this human lifetime. There is no time like the present.

The presence is the power of you.

So it is, and so mote it be!

Chapter 7

SPIRITUAL PHARMACY

SOUL PRESCRIPTION

I AM, the best version of me and myself in perfect alignment. I am a beacon of light that fuels the divine flame within, if and when I feel the adverse of this...its negativity, so I go check into the Universe, for a prescription of positivity and dose up on all the self-care and self-love, nurturing thyself, honouring thyself, loving thyself, this is the best universal medicine. I owe it to ME, the most important person. The divine nectar the soul craves and deserves, is a dose of tonic to replenish positivity, and balance the power! May all my days be a constant stream of wellbeing, endless love, blessings and positivity.

So it is, and so mote it be!

Vacations and holiday retreat gives a time out, a time to just wind down, relax and enjoy. We feel our best and happiest dependant on the experience. However not everyone will have this opportunity due to individual circumstances. It really doesn't matter, what is relevant is how you take the time out to self-nurture, self-care, self-love for the optimal well-being of yourself. You owe that to you!

Attempt to set an intention as a part of a routine in resonance of life. This practice will impact your mental well-being state to set the tone for the rest of the day, week etc. Resonating with serenity, tranquillity and peacefulness will benefit you in ways unexpected. You will be surprised by the extraordinary opportunities, and satisfying achievements.

Today Declare: *I am grateful for the day ahead…I saturate the whole of my day with peace, joy, love & contentment and it is done!*

Why is it such a struggle when anyone is faced with a change. There is resistant that persists, one is so entrapped in a comfort zone and to move beyond this creates this reluctance, be it through fear or lack of self-esteem. A transition necessitates the growth required for the next phase of transformation. It becomes such a power struggle from within, that you are fighting yourself and not opening up to the revelations that come about as you progress the next step.

Challenges are meant to be uncomfortable; it is an opportunity to heal wounds that have become so stagnant and stuck. A process of elimination is necessary for the next stage of growth, which cannot happen until we are prepared to take the steps. Vacations/holiday breaks and any medical prescriptions is only sugar coating and plastering the wounds into a suppression and not a release. When one truly honours a sacredness towards themselves, and truly valuing themselves, will feel the magical possibilities that start to unfold and deliver results far beyond any expectation.

It's pertinent that you delve deeply to connect with what resonates with you most, and then move forward to the next step of what you are trying to accomplish, and how you can achieve that in the moment.

When we are not in alignment of our desires or values in the way we want to achieve them, we will have a different view or approach, therefore it's imperative to understand what is in the best balance between the two things that makes sense forthcoming.

Your body is more than often ignored when it is trying to get your attention, it will be speaking to you through the physical system producing sensations to bring alertness. It's almost like advance subtle warnings that if you do not heed any calling or response to the presented physical symptoms, then they are more than likely to escalate or exacerbate the symptoms, that's when it becomes a problem.

This magnificent phenomenal system's performance, can be overlooked and taken for granted by many. Optimise its performance by connecting with your network of communication channels. Think of all the technical issues relating PC's, TV's, wi fi. The signals can sometimes have an interruption for a smooth flowing operation, yet you will be asserting your dominance towards a more efficient, stable and reliable solution for a problem, before it completely fails or breakdown. Why cannot the same principles apply to your physical energy system. It is after all consistently operating if not to its maximum potential, it is still continuously serving you. Why not just take a brief pause, and ask your physical;

"How may I assist you to achieve the best possible outcome for whatever it is presented to you in any given moment"

Honour your physical, delve into, and connect consciously to your mind to find the best possible solution for your problem.

Dear higher self I am feeling the effects of dysfunction on my physical health, what is the message that I need to understand about this. Just pause and see what needs focus:

Here is a list of brief examples:

Feet~ indicates an imbalance, not a weakness. Are you grounded, stable and secure, to stand up for yourself firmly without fear of falling down.

Knees~ are hurting: denotes are you struggling to walk your path: what is inhibiting your knees from moving forward with your life trajectory, due to stiffness, pain~ the inventory of proceeding forward to the next step.

Backpain~ relates to your support system. Don't bend over backwards for the sake of your own health for others if the reciprocation is not forthcoming or lacking towards you.

Hips/Pelvis~ stability. Are you firmly held together to heed your commands

Ankles~ weakness to handle firm stance of predicament in your life

Arms- are you rising to the challenges or falling down, are you moving forward or backwards, are you retreating inwards or outwards to make progress in your daily routine or actions

Hands~ are you afraid of handling or gripping the situation of the present circumstances you fear.

Wrists~ are you open and flexible towards your own needs.

Shoulders~ what are you burdened with that needs to be offloaded. That saying "the weight of the world on your shoulders" is apt when it comes to your shoulders.

Neck~ rotation. What is stuck that you are not able to move forward, or take direction or change what is not working.

Eyes~ clarity and vision for your purpose, if it's not clear, then open up to what you need to focus to get a clearer picture of your vision and goals

Mouth~ what are you taking in that is digesting or diluting your body to the point that your brain doesn't know what you're talking about or what you're saying.

Throat~ expression of yourself. Is speech stuck, altered or is there a breakdown in communication.

Nose~ breathe not smell, sense of what feels good and flows through you and your mind and body as well as well as your perception

Head- your thoughts, your mind, feelings and emotions ~ clear the mental clutter and headspace for smooth operation of the body

Legs- are you striding forward or backwards, or just stuck in your present state of flow.

Viewing the exterior can be an aesthetic or cosmetic effect, sometimes the deeper services one can give to oneself, is to focus within to the interior engine.

Embrace change to live with intention and purpose, you will be surprised with the potentials it offers. By exploring something new, you will be surprised how easy it becomes and what you learn from such experiences. Just taking the initial step towards something new, and the unknown will yield results that you will be surprised by. Just trust and mostly honour this time out for you, it is sacred for you, and a catalyst for soul evolution. Taking this time out, you get to explore the depth of the soul of you, to the root of the matter, by facing your shadows, this darkness that is the doing of your own doubts and fears, release what is not of purpose or serves soul growth, and unlock the infinite possibilities of profound healing naturally, it will empower you for sure!

I have seen astounding results time and time again when individuals have attended my meditation or healing sessions. The phenomenal changes from their first attendance flourishes them onwards to a changed vibrant, positive being with a different mindset. My heart just swells to witness such changes, and is consistently the best antidote for my soul. I am in awe and so grateful, and blessed, but mostly honoured for all my gifts of healing abilities. I am so "Thankful" to the Universe, for bestowing these gifts of services, which I am profoundly passionate, humbled and above all honoured to do God's work, feeling completely blessed. Life is a treasure, talents are a gift, being of service is a joy, and an utter true enlightenment. A journey becomes fulfilling and satisfying, when one truly serves within their true authentic higher self!

Intent on making what is unfamiliar, familiar with the introduction of something new, breaking free from a comfort zone that restricts and impedes growth. How you value yourself will determine how you honour yourself too. Be sincere to oneself to let go of what is not in your optimum health and well-being of your evolvement. The only limiting growth aspect of yourself will be the old self that is set in such ways. The emergence of YOU births in radiance and recognition. Note the importance of "**R**" letter here.

The ever-flowing constant cycle of life is renewal and revival= transformation. Are you ready to reclaim your vitality. Take a moment to reflect from the presence to the way forward, detach from the past pathways, and release what no longer serves or enhances you i.e. stubborn old patterns, stubborn attachments, old ties, oppressive behaviours and fears. In sincerity of being the free spirit of your soul that you are meant to be. The purpose of you being on earth is to be HAPPY... happiness is fuelled by LOVE....this is the energy that your soul thrives on, this is your existence, the energy of the Universe. Make a restart of a new cycle of beginnings, the power of the new you rising through the turbulence of any emotions that leads to a space of authentic presence. Life after all is what you make it! Time to shut those old doors down and move forward with strength irrespective of the resistance. Allow yourself with ease and gentleness to move through any triggers, repel the negatives with the positives to thrive again, the outcome of a perfect resolution.

If this doesn't compel you to make any radical changes for restoration of YOU, then not only are you in denial, but sacrificing self at the detriment of living and embodying the truth of who you are, and for what you truly deserve.

Are you ready to bask in the glorious super light from within, in all its purity, to activate all that was already there to its natural wholesome pureness, that got lost and indented through programs of life school by human directives.

Then commence to check into the Universe, for your spiritual prescription, available only from the Spiritual Pharmacy.

Ensure your spiritual prescription consists of:

Radiance, Recognition, Renewal, Revival, Reclaim, Reflect, Release, Restart, Resistance and Resolution.

Daily Dose

Signed: *The Universe*

Date: *The presence*

Dispensed by: *The Spiritual Pharmacy.*

The health benefits:
- *Empowerment (power; strength, strong)*
- *Self Esteem (self-confidence; motivated, willpower)*
- *Gratitude (thankful for all lessons & blessings)*
- *Bounce back from challenges (growth)*
- *Vibrant (full of energy & life)*
- *Awareness (of self; thoughts, actions)*
- *Happiness (contentment & fulfilment)*
- *Stress free (peace, worry free, clarity, positive outlook)*

Possible side effects:
- *reinforce new neural pathways in your brain that eventually become automatic processes.*
- *Decreasing of stress chemical Cortisol when we think happy thoughts or feel joy*
- *Increasing of serotonin in response to our positive emotions.*
- *Optimism makes it easier to avoid worry and negative thinking*
- *Coping better with Stress*
- *Greater feelings of happiness and overall satisfaction with life*

Adverse effects:
- *Engaging in repetitive old bad habits and patterns. ...*
- *Not learning from mistakes. ...*
- *Inability to change thought process ...*
- *Inability to process emotions. ...*
- *Being inauthentic. ...*
- *Failing to self-care, self-love ...*
- *Ignoring warning signs.*

The Spiritual Pharmacy Aftercare Advice

Gratitude: *Each day, awaken to greet your day with gratitude, allow this to be a momentum of an unfolding day to commence to the tune of whatever is representing to the highest tone and frequency, of your thought in that present moment.*

Connect: *Resonate with the feeling from that thought, to allow the theme of that, to set the tone of what it is to be, in a positive flow and vibrancy and not anything else.*

Advocate: *"I AM" in charge, "I AM" responsible for* ME, *don't victimise oneself, this is not God honouring of thyself. Look who you are, a wonderful masterpiece and creation, yet it is not shining and flowing to the being of oneself.*

Now go seize your day!

Think of a Rainbow, I have not known anyone to criticise a Rainbow when it appears, if anything, it energetically draws attention to the colours and the arch. Utter astonishment, smiles and positive comments. Even an image of it in mindset alters one's vibration in that moment.

Stride your being, like a rainbow; each colour hues magical and uplifting, reflecting the mode of ones being, magically transformed. The highest honour and esteem one can award itself is recognition of thyself. Don't be clouded in judgement of what is not...it is at your own will, you can overcome, and it is at your own will you can destruct. Life can be assembled, and put together like a jigsaw puzzle to create an amazing piece of accomplishment. You just have to look within, and piece what needs to mould together and the rest is a flow.

If you are rooted and grounded in life (red colour), would be indicative of this. Which incidentally relates to the earth chakra known as Root Chakra - is all things connected to earth, indicative of how we make a living- material life, abundance and finances. Growth of anything uproots from the seedlings of whatever we nurture, and sow in life. If we tend to seeds, nurture from ground up, we will have the results for our efforts on life. That is the embodiment of how you necessitate the growth. If you just expect it will happen itself, the results would be different to the efforts if you tended to it.

I recall one morning as I awoke and uttered "Thank You Universe" I imagined a shining rainbow archway, and instinctively gravitated towards the colour yellow. This energy centre is the solar plexus chakra which indicates I need to focus on my power centre today, my self-esteem, my confidence. So, today the choice is not to be in victimisation of oneself in lacking mode, but to take charge to focus on the positive steps to an unfoldment of a tone to set the day.

Today Declare: *I chose to praise myself and sent gratitude of huge thankfulness, for all my blessings that the Universe would bestow upon me. I stand in my power of me. I am positive and confident in all that arises today to handle with strength and vigour.*

I was also talking myself out of doing my daily practice of yoga, as I didn't feel like it, I didn't feel like doing anything. I was in a kind of feel sorry for me mood, and other excuses! However, I chose to take the strength to be confident enough, to attempt my daily morning yoga session, as this was going to help enormously to loosen all my back and shoulder muscles to be pain free. I instilled in my mindset the positive effects from this were going to offset my mood and pain to make a huge difference.

I greeted my day to honour my vessel with healthy food choices, this is the tonic that the soul nourishes and my vessel heals from. No excuses as I can do it!

I will focus on the necessary positive steps to be in MY power.

As the day flowed, I was awarded with a feeling of "feel good factor" throughout from the accomplishments of tasks succeeded and attempted.

It's similar scenario to having all the ingredients and instructions to bake or cook a perfect meal, dessert, to sew or knit, assemble a piece of furniture. The same applies to your daily day, set the tone, place the steps, to achieve the perfect outcome. Without the instructions and intentions, you know the outcome of the flow....

You want the perfect dinner, date, Christmas, new year, birthday, holiday, the list just becomes endless… why not just a life that is perfect to your needs....it's not hard...its misunderstood.

The chakras, specifically the 7 on our physical (etheric) body, are pure energy vortex wheels, and refers to energy points in the body that spin at a speed for harmonious balance, if they are unbalanced it would indicate they are blocked. They correspond to bundles of nerves, major organs, and areas of our energetic body that affect our emotional and physical well-being. Each Chakra has a colour, a purpose, and association to an area of our life.

CHARKAS	COLOUR	ELEMENT	LOCATED	SYMBOL	Represents
ROOT/BASE	Red	Earth	base of spine between genitals		our foundation stone upon which we build. Its main themes are grounding, family, material life and security. We must feel safe and have our basic needs met (food/shelter), otherwise we are still in survival consciousness or fear state.
SACRAL	Orange	Water	Below navel		It is associated creativity, pleasure, and sexuality, **governs the experience for our lives through feelings and sensations.** It›s the center of emotion, pleasure, enjoyment, sensuality, intimacy, and connection
SOLAR PLEXUS	Yellow	Fire	Above navel		a center of personal strength, learning and comprehension. It guides you through life by creating a strong sense of self, setting personal boundaries and building self-esteem and willpower. The ability to bring change into your life

HEART	Green	Air	Centre of Chest		The fundamental qualities are pure, unconditional love and compassion. It is through the Heart chakra that we become confident, secure, morally responsible and at its core, this chakra is emotional and propels us to enhance our emotional development.
THROAT	Pale Blue	Ether	Between Inner Colloarbone		Is responsible for communication, self-expression, the ability to speak your personal truth. It can be used to create anything you want in life.
THIRD EYE	Indigo	All elements	Between the eyes		It is the centre of insight, consciousness and intuition, and mysticism. The third eye is the sixth out of seven chakras that control the meridian of the body, mind, and spirit. It can take us to a place of higher consciousness and enlightenment.

CROWN	Violet, white, Gold	All elements	Top centre of Head		Is all about spiritual connection, a higher purpose, to something greater than ourselves, a sense of cosmic consciousness, connecting you to the divine (angelic energy, the Source, Creator or God.) This chakra also gives you a sense of your own supreme self-divinity, become more selfless and compassionate, an awareness that you are a soul in a human body.

The colours of the rainbow depict the colours of the chakras:

Chapter 8

GRIEF

BIRTH, SOUL, DEATH (BSD)

Grief....is not always about the loss we endure of a loved one, but all that we have imbedded throughout life. The memories are just some parts of it, it's also all that we have absorbed through our physical, it's what's retained in our emotional and mental bodies. The physical will present the visible symptoms of sadness, tears, anger, or whatever behaviour is your way of dealing with such circumstances.

Our powerful mind, is our mental body, the storage compartment of all memories, the good, the bad and the ugly...the latter would be the trauma...we all take our trip down to memory lane of happier times, fond memories and they make us smile as they are recalled. The bad and ugly would be the sad, upsetting traumatic memories that get tucked away in our cellular memory through the emotional body. The organs, the heart, tissues and our muscles, all too often, we either forgot or are too absorbed by the trigger points that set off the memory behaviours. Have we ever just paused...to just reflect what our own body our physical is telling us. Even I as an experienced professional therapist, just dealt with grief as just the loss, not the impact of the story on one's physical. Our physical isn't just the body. It's our 4body system, made up of our physical body, emotional body, mental body and spiritual body.

Often enough you find those, that have been given a prognosis of terminal illness, there isn't a get out ticket available, therefore they have to, at some point come to terms and as soon as they do, the aspect of their spiritual body comes into play to offset the behaviour pattern to resonate with the emotional and mental body.

The sync will always be out, because in any situation not all of the 4body system comes into play in a perfect balance. The equilibrium and balance is always out of sync.

Inevitably one always attaches the advection aspect of grief solely on the actual loss, not on the layers and layers of pain, sadness and heartache.

One can truly understand grief if they have gone through a personal loss, otherwise all one can do is empathise, and join in through the feelings and the emotions it creates, and be absorbed in the wavelength of the sadness and emptiness it creates.

A loss of a loved one is unbearable, and coming to terms takes a process through healing day by day. Eventually we have to come to an acceptance, but this itself is a process on an individual basis. Every genetic being is different, and one cannot step to ease, rush, smother or comfort this process. Each one is at their own individual pace.

I endured three huge personal losses of loved ones in my life, my younger brother, my father, and then followed my mother. I know they are in a better place, and their soul is basking eternally in unconditional love, beyond immeasurable and a glorious light thriving their spiritual aspect of being. It is those that are left behind, you and me, and all those affected that cannot comprehend or begin to understand the extent of a loss on a mortal level. One day the inevitable is going to happen to each one of us, no one lives forever. It is just a continuous chain, a link that breaks away, until such a time you connect that link when you return to be with them. The chain will always continue making more links as the family extends further in the line of this chain. A link is detached but it is also re connected to the missing link, this is the continuity of an ancestral line. It is never broken, just detached.

Nothing is lost forever; nothing ever stops either. One may take pit a stop or a pause on their journey of life here on this earth plane, but the route of one's destination has to continue. We all have one path, individual journeys, experiences and lessons as a part of our divine plan. An ancestral line never stops or ends – the chain, it continues on. The link that detached will appear for the connection, when you yourself get the call home to the heavenly plane.

My brother's death in 2016, was unexpected and the acceptance was surreal, the loss was unbearable, but eventually through the reality of what had happened you find a way to go on living without that individual, until such a time you accept the parting has happened and is permanent. Realistically my personal experience and I am sure for many, the first twelve months are challenging. In the first year you go through the motions and memories of this time yesterday, last week, last month, last year, the birthday, Christmas, anniversary, easter, summer holidays etc, every event will flood the memories to that time of what you were doing together. Until you have completed a full twelve-month cycle, and approach the next year, you don't really have the memories or comparisons to make of the year before, as that's the time you were in your grieving process of the parting, and the undeniable loss. You never get over a loss, but find your way through healing of oneself by getting through and treasuring the memories.

My father's death was inevitable, I thought in those four years he fought a horrendous battle to live, and continuously survived despite professional medical opinions. I was living through this process with him, and had thought I was indeed prepared for the eventuality. I often said I was already grieving, my dad a beautiful soul had a fighting warrior spirit within him to survive, until such a time the body just gave up, although his mindset was strong. This loss and parting broke my heart, but I found a resilience within me, as I had witnessed his unbearable pain, and suffering for 4 long years, and he was now finally out of this, no longer suffering, this was what gave me peace. As a spiritual healer I am only too aware that life does continue, and I do get a lot of signs from my dad, who was also a very spiritual man himself, and helped a lot of people throughout his life. Spiritually I am aware he is still very much around watching over me, and my daughter. However, I am human and have to submit myself to the feelings and emotions as and when they hit. It's at times like this, I sob my heart out as I miss his physical aspect, his words of wisdom, his infectious laugh and humbleness and above all his love. A big part of my dearest Popsie, is within me in a hugely genetic way, his blood runs through my veins, and I have certain attributes of him too.

I know his love will always stay with me through all those precious memories, but mostly his blessings. This is one of the biggest parting gifts he bestowed upon me, and for that I am forever eternally in gratitude.

So, I guess I totally understand the reason why this book was delayed, which I thought were and probably to some extent were excuses. This book was birthed now, and not written when I had initially planned for it, because further knowledge and wisdom had to be attained, which came about through this grieving process of my dad, my world, my everything.

In January 2021 I channelled the below message:

Healing through words will touch the nation, yet there is still so much to do. The impact of your words will touch souls to impact a shift by means of healing. You will be guided and not on your own...there are many that support you on this mission, a team awaits for that right time. You seem to think you are ready, but yet you too need to be healed from the wounds of the past to transcend and transition forward. Dearest one, what we see is that you are weary, this is not the vibration to evoke such connections, all will be revealed in perfect divine order. It is and will be within reach to that spectrum for revelation. This is your own turmoil and dilemma that is commanded from the mind, as it pressures oneself into thinking what it deems is right for you. Breathe into your prana to rain the reality of the intelligence of what is. You have that access, but first you must be in alignment of such frequency to gain access of what is already there. You have that imbedded within.

I ask please can my guides name be revealed that support me on this earthly mission?

This too will be revealed when you are in that frequency through your alignment, all in divine timing. I know I am impatient. But surely this is coming through from someone?

Today whilst writing this, I am easily finding excuses for not doing my yoga practice, listening to the mind, do it tomorrow, start tomorrow it's a better day....my body is already subjected to feeling tired as this is what the mind thinks the body needs...I have been awake since 4am and now I need sleep.... the question is, I can easily obey because I agree and know it's right.... I am now in awareness; it is at this point I have control. What do I do.... take control...diversify to overcome....omg!! My eyes are feeling very heavy, so much to the point that it is so easy just to shut and fall asleep, even to the point of convincing myself it is what I need, yes when I get up I will do my yoga...yet again the presentation will be to divert from the intention or desire because the mind will present what it deems the body needs.... What did I do?

Pleased to say I did an intense yoga workout....bravo me!! Manipulate or trick our way out from the comfort zone....

My wish for you my reader, if you have endured a loss, that you too also find some comfort and, healing through these words of wisdom, to get you through a parting and or an undeniable loss you may have felt or are feeling. My dad's initials were B.S.D- so in his honour and memory, this chapter is dedicated to him and my mom, symbolising that as Birth, Soul, Death= BSD, and my mom's name started with a S and family surname D, therefore the whole initials BSD is a family dedication.

The universal flow is energy that exists within you, the vibrational stance or wavelength you operate from. Your being operates from this mass energy system. Your breath, the life force of all being, your heartbeat, the engine system in your brain- your mind, that orchestrates and collaborates with the body your vehicle, your organs are all the parts to function the body, your food is the fuel to run the body, and your circulation is all blood and water to keep the wavelength flowing.

Become aware of what an amazing system we have, we take our vessel for granted. The partnership it has to optimise a state of order, through the choice or decision made. We are blessed with such a smart operative system; we have the controls to direct how it runs through the conveyance of our messages. We could have a smooth perfect system or one that causes havoc. Which would you prefer and opt for? Only you are responsible for self and your life, no other, just YOU.

BIRTH- when one arrives on the earth plane birthed to the chosen parents, there is joy, happiness, celebration, a coming together. An exuberance of exhilaration and excitement of a new family member, a link connected to the parents through the ancestral chain.

SOUL- the exterior is a beautiful aspect of the physical to see, our human self. Within is our temple and there resides our beautiful soul. The energy of creation to infuse and activate this physical aspect of you for growth and development, and evolvement. Activation of energy system- movement and breath. The mind is activated, a clean slate/platform with no data. Ready to commence storage of life experiences and lessons.

DEATH- the extraction of the four-body energy system and soul departure. Awakening the spirit of your soul on the heavenly realm, a spiritual awakening- the higher aspect of your being awakened in pure consciousness-it is this aspect of our being that continues on. De-activation of energy system- stillness. The mind is deactivated- conscious matter merges towards higher consciousness- data starts to delete through process of elimination through soul extraction.

We are all energy and our being consists of; The four-body energy system; the physical body- sensory, the emotional body- feelings, the mental body- thoughts and spiritual body- consciousness. Each activating and de activating our being.

JIMBO

On the 4th September 2016, my dearest sweetest younger brother jimmy, a beautiful soul with a huge heart of gold, left his earthly incarnation to go home. We had an amazing close relationship from childhood, the funs, the laughter, and so much more. I always looked out for him at school, being his elder sister. He was just one of a kind, the sweetest, kindest and humbling soul. Never took anything seriously. He truly understood life as just living in every joyous, happiest moment. There were never any dull moments with him, just happiness, so much love and lots of laughter. So many people from all walks of life just gravitated towards him, and absolutely adored him. Oh, beautiful gentle one how our hearts were ripped out that morning. I questioned all my faith and spirituality and really vented my anger at it. What was the use, I didn't care at this point. I just wanted my brother back, not just for me but for his young family too. It just wasn't fair!

My whole world just seemed to collapse in front of me. Me and the rest of my family were not prepared for this or least expected it. But only our creator knows when it is time to come home, and so he was called back and left us all without a goodbye or so we thought at that time.

It was already challenging, grieving the loss of giving my only child away to marital bliss, even though this was a sense of a positive grieving. I certainly didn't ask the universe for a double whammy! Thank you, Universe! It was a lovely stress to deal with the wedding of my only child but little did I know what was about to follow on from this. How was it possible to be honoured the most joyous, happiest time of celebrations one weekend, and then the following weekend it is all taken away, and to be thrown into the depths of grieving and mourning. Happiness then sadness, oh yes the yin and yang was in balance but not in the way I desired.

I guess I was sort of preparing for my elderly parents, everyone does, as it is inevitable, and that it will happen at some point one day. The sorrow and grieving wouldn't have been any less, but at least it's a mental preparation, but not only that, you know by that time or age they would have experienced their life to that point. But not for my younger brother, taken so suddenly and unexpectedly. All questions I fired were blank answers, for someone who had so much to live for and to see his children grow up, marry and have children of their own one day….everything taken from them too!

Life itself challenges to the many aspects of who you truly are; sometimes it is the biggest challenges that will test our faith of being and the existence of us, me, you, all. I thought I had endured enough of what had already evolved me as a person. There never was once a doubt once I had grown to, what I thought made me the individual to whom I was. Strong, confident, passionate and most importantly spiritual. I truly loved me and what I was all about, turbulence and all. OMG! How wrong was I. On that day I became a weak melting broken soul, in heart and mind, completely inconsolable.

"love you jimbo"

DAD

On 21st July 2020 my dearest beloved father left his earthly incarnation for the higher realms. It was inevitable it was going to happen one day, but no matter how prepared you think you are; it still is a painful acceptance and process.

We had an amazing father/daughter relationship and openly discussed anything and everything even death and its process. Our spiritual conversations were very therapeutic, my dad always commented this as 'satsang' (a word from the Sanskrit which means to associate with true people or be in the company of true people).

When we had these very deep conversations, we were always oblivious of time, it just didn't exist, to the point when these conversations ended it felt like an almighty powerful session! Sometimes you could feel the energies of Ascended masters and deities amongst you, that had joined in for the enlightened experience.

I am indeed grateful for all the time we had, and although I accept as a spiritual being that life continues on, I do sometimes have to retract to my human self and have my bouts of emotions. I know he is with me but I do miss his physical presence sorely, the hugs and 'I love you' and all the words of wisdom we shared with each other. I know for a fact he is guiding me from up above, yet I feel the empty void on a human level. I am at peace though, knowing his suffering is over. The agonising long 4 years of excruciating pain and suffering to finally release from the vessel that contained his soul. My father had an amazing fighting warrior soul to continuously fight his way for his life, he certainly had more than 9 lives of a cat! Despite the very medical professional writing him off, time and time again over the 4 years, he bounced back! They were just shocked, surprised and duped because he surpassed and survived every damn expectation, to the point 2 years previous palliative care was being discussed and arranged. Medics are focused to scientific proven methods as opposed to spiritual and positive mindsets. I guess also on the same token dad still had lessons to endure. Your last breath was not done until God ordered it, all in divine timing, not a moment sooner or a moment later, just precise in his will and beckon, the call home. The years that poppy lived was a testament to his determination to exceed what the medical expectation was, being a very wise and spiritual soul, he definitely had this unique warrior strength of steel within him, his tenacity to outlive the many expectations imposed on him over and over again. During those 4 years I cared for my father, and looking back I am grateful I had that honour of service towards his time of need, nothing can replace the hard work and caring duties I fulfilled until his very last breath in my hands. I am honoured and privileged to have humbly served him throughout. *"Dearest poppy you are finally free beautiful soul, my life will never be the same without you, your love and much more. I know you are in eternal bliss finally home. I love you my dad, my rock, my everything until we meet again".*

1st Birthday without Dad

My birthday in 2020, without both parents! Mum was in hospital, two days prior she was rushed into hospital with declining health.

Bless her! she never forgot my birthday, the last couple years she has just been so lost in her own world from vascular dementia that followed on from her major stroke. She doesn't exist in any time frame presently. I didn't envisage how this day was going to plan out, but it was already planned by divine intervention, so I could have a day to myself without all the full on 24hr caring duties. Nevertheless, I awoke to being in gratitude, and determined that today was going to be positive, and specifically so in memory of my dearest poppy too! I spent my last birthday with him last year, and the memories and the beautiful photo of me and him just evoked many emotions of missing him dearly, even though I am fully aware he is living life in god's kingdom. My humanness just decided to step in today.

1st Christmas without Dad:

Christmas 2020 was a surreal experience, specifically with current covid restrictions in place, for me on a personal level it was the first Christmas without my dearest dad. He loved Christmas; it was his favourite season. I was just not in the mood for the festivities as it evoked so many memories, however to honour my dad's memory, I did put up his tree and felt a sense of his presence from doing this, this gave me a lot of comfort and peace, each day I looked at the tree and it just made Christmas flow, which was surprising! What I did not envisage or expect was the turmoil of emotions that were to erupt straight after Christmas. Each day I cried my heart out, sometimes 2-3 times a day. Omg! What was going on, previously whenever I cried, I released and felt at peace, but this was something different. Just a memory, his photo or a piece of music just set me off. I put it down to his birthday, which was on New Year's Day 1st January, a first birthday of many many more without him. This was difficult, yet once New year arrived, I felt at peace. I reflected on the week past and the turbulence of emotions and concluded it was a healing that was taking effect releasing the stored grief, cleansing the heart, mind and body, ready for the new platform ahead.

The year 2020 has been a difficult year for many worldwide with the corona virus, so to greet 2021 was in anticipation, as more and more announcements came for further lockdowns! Aside from that we were moving from a 3dimensional way of life into the 5th dimension. This alone would bring up a lot of egoic stuff that cannot exist or allow you to merge into the 5D.

Although the festive season was tough as both my parents loved Christmas. I did manage to get through with acceptance that 'popsie' is now at peace and pain free with no more suffering. I did still get the odd waves of emotions that suddenly came up from nowhere and hit me, resorting me to just release and release and empty out. As a spiritual lightworker, you have this level of understanding that life does continue on, I guess it's all the physical aspect that you dearly miss.

Although the year 2020 has been a surreal kind of year for all, most with various personal losses, and others just the unfolding of what was and what is and what will be.

I was also presently in the throes of witnessing a downward spiral in my dearest loving mother, who became a former shell of herself. Two strokes, progressive vascular dementia, and the loss of her dearest beloved husband, soul mate. She absolutely loved and adored my father so much, to the extent that this was so evident in her persona. She grieved and cried out for him. Although with such ailing and complicated health issues, to me she was displaying heavy symptoms of being heartbroken, and this is what seems to impact and exacerbate, and accelerate her current health issues to a point of no return.

It was difficult and hard to watch her daily letting go, just giving up. Having no fight left in her tender vessel and soul. I just came to expect the unexpected, and what I witnessed was not my mother but a very weak, tired soul. My mother was a fiercely independent sociable loving being, she fully enjoyed life and her social circles, very outgoing and independent. Everyone not just immediate family but extended circles loved my mum, she like my dearest father, did a lot of good for a lot of people, and it's so comforting to hear all this as a part of the healing process too. In this cruel illness she is just so lost, wherever she is...just becoming lifeless, it's easier said that she was just becoming a vegetable, but she wasn't that, she was a human being with a lost soul. This was not the mum I knew, she's became a vulnerable child in an adult vessel, so for now it's all about just being with her, showering her with love and more love, just creating a space of so much unconditional love, support and comfort until it is time the call home comes.

I prayed to source, God and the Angels, her suffering completes without pain, and be a peaceful transition. She doesn't deserve this, I guess no one ever does but sometimes the route to exit the earth planes can become very unbearable to witness, let alone experience it from the viewpoint of the individual who is actually going through it!

This phase can drag out or end abruptly but it is nevertheless unpleasant...I came to accept and know what was ahead...

Clearing & releasing the past, that no longer serves my highest good, embracing my way forward to all new beginnings. Shedding the old self, making way for new change, direction, transformation. Through the darkness comes the infinite light with new possibilities in perfect alignment of my antenna to God/Universe in the beautiful energies of the way forward.

Blessed are those that bring blessings unto others. All is insignificant when eventually the reality of what was and what is, is now significant. When we are in amidst of something, we are not in realisation or awake, we most certainly are oblivious, to the point that when we look back, we finally awaken and take note that amidst those episodes of tornados there were many blessings too. This is expressing to our knowledge that the pace of life just becomes too serious to a point that we miss moments of living. We are engulfed in the surroundings of what is unfolding rather than flowing. Why does it take a parting whether it is death, divorce or separation etc that we are fighting against the flow, rather than being with the flow of life.

1st Father's Day without my darling Pops!

I LOVE YOU SO MUCH DAD! Miss you too much, what keeps me going is knowing you are in a far much better place, no more suffering. You are free from all the pains and suffering from your earthly life and vessel. Your soul is residing in the highest ranks of where it belongs for all the good you did here. I am so proud of your mission, lessons and challenges. I'm so proud that I am, was and continue to be your daughter. Your blood runs through my veins! We were one of a kind, we understood each other. My life and my heart will never be the same without you!! I miss you so much, and always remember you saying "when I'm not here, just close your eyes and I will be standing next to you. I wish I could see you but I can't, I know that it's maybe I'm trying too hard, and too absorbed in my emotions and not letting go. I look forward to the day we meet again. My love for you will always continue in my heart and my memories. I do hope this heavy heart of mine heals, and I continue to make you proud of me

I love you 'popsie'. Never forgotten always treasured

There will be a time in your journey when the time comes, and you snap out of the mindset that you seem to inadvertently think is the right way, irrespective of what you believe is the right way. To give you a personal experience from my own is 'that what you think you know is not what you think you need' but more so what you believe you are, and deserving off, because it is your birth right! I am deserving of this as I am honouring my needs. What I give is what I receive. Life just doesn't happen, every step taken is a route to somewhere to gain something, we are nothing yet we are also everything. When we birthed into this earth plane, the most powerful precious aspect was YOU… the soul within the vessel that was created. This creation started a long time before the predicted pregnancy term of 9 months! And arriving on this mighty planet to your chosen parent/s.

The same applies when you return back to your creator to the heavenly plane, the soul/spirit returns home without the vessel, with all the lessons and experiences…a story, a tapestry of your life. What's left behind is your vessel, the family, friends, personal belongings, money etc. Nothing goes with you; so, what makes perfect sense is not always adhered to, and that is to find the joy of living your life in every moment. Majority just forget to live, and just exist. Only you are a testament to self of the perfect embodiment of all that you are through the "I am". I am a mighty author of my life; we are all authors because we are writing our own life story. You came as a blank page, but return with chapter and verse of a lifetime of your earthly life. How you go is not in your hands, but how you commence your journey and proceed through is.

Mom

On 3rd September 2022, my dearest sweetest mother, left her earthly incarnation for the higher realms. Oh my! what another strong warrior spirit, she endlessly fought her way back from brink of death each time. There was a fighting spirit within her to live, and she always said she wasn't ready to go, despite what the palliative team and doctors predicted. Even to the point when she saw spirit approaching her, she would shout "Go away, I'm not ready yet!" this pretty much went on for at least 18months.

Me and my mom didn't have a close relationship, it was kind of a love hate relationship, however when she became ill in 2018, we became very close and particularly so in the last 2years of her life, after poppy passed. Oh my days, I loved her fiercely and became considerably protective of her. It was almost like a role reversal; she became my baby and I the mother. Every day, I would tell her how much I loved her, and when she was able, she would say it to me too. The cruel disease took mom away long before she passed. Visually she was my mom but mentally she was a vulnerable child. There were no more conversations, each week leading up to her death, she became more and more frail. It was unbearable to watch as well as heart-breaking.

Week leading to her death, there were unusual activity happening. I guess when I look back it was all the signs spirit were sending. On the Sunday, both my mum's carers approached me, feeling unsure how to tell me, that they had found white feathers in her bed, as well as one on top of the duvet. They were surprised as there were no cushions around her, which would be explainable. Then on the Monday afternoon as I sat down next to mum's bed, I happened to glance at the huge window, and noticed a beautiful white feather floating outside, it put a smile on my face.

I always slept on a sofa next to my mum's bed. On the following night, as I fell asleep, I was awoken by voices, someone having full blown conversation. It was 2.30am, I briefly opened my eyes to see who had come into the room, there was no one there. I dropped back off to sleep, the conversations started again. Obviously, there were no neighbours, as we were in a rural location, no one in the room, so I just put it down to spirit and spiritual conversations. On the Wednesday night, again as I fell asleep, I was awoken by a beaming light sparkling onto my face. It felt like someone had a torch and switching it on and off directly on my face. When I opened my eyes there was no one there, as I attempted to close my eyes again, I noticed the balcony roof window, and the beam was coming from there. As I went up the stairs, and got closer to the window I saw a huge glowing shining star. It blinked 3times, I was amazed and turned to look down on mum, then back, and the star had disappeared. I made my way back down and kept staring towards the window to see if would come back again, it didn't. On Thursday evening as the Carers were attending to my mum, I stepped out the room to bring my mum's fresh laundry in. As I came back into the room, I started to speak to the Carers, and at this point, my mum heard my voice and turned her head round, and opened her eyes and looked straight at me. She hadn't opened her eyes for a month, this was a miracle. I was ecstatic, I dropped the laundry and ran up to her, and hugged her, kissed her and cried at the same time, as well as repeating 'I love you mum, I love you mum' Just as suddenly as she had opened her eyes, she closed them too. It is at this point I felt a huge pang in my heart. Mum was saying 'Goodbye' The fulfilment of our mother daughter soul contract had come to an end. She didn't open her eyes again, despite my brother and daughter coming into the room. It was hard to witness as they pleaded so much. I knew this was only for me, but I was saddened for my brother and my daughter who both were immensely close to mum too. On that night the whole family, myself, my daughter, brother, his wife and children as well as the grandchildren all stayed in the room with mum. Having conversations, laughing joking and watching wedding films of both mum and dad. The atmosphere was full of love and joy. The following day my mother passed away peacefully surrounded with so much love in the room. Final goodbye's are never easy but the atmosphere of peace and love was what soothed everyone. There were tears and there was sadness.

I was absolutely overwhelmed by the comments from carers, nurses, palliative team about how much care that had been dedicated to mum, and it was because of this commitment and love, she had lasted as long as she had. It was the greatest honour for me to serve my mum in her time of need. She bought me into this world, with that same dedication, love and adoration, and I gave back what she deserved and much more when she left this world. I also need to commend my brother as without him, the last eight months of mum's life, we were there for her together in solidarity.

Dearest Dad, Mom, & Jimbo, in sweetest memory of you I dedicate:

"Today I focus on Love, this is the epitome of all our being. I honour what we had by invoking love, within the depths of my heart. The scars in my heart heal through this love, in my heart is where you reside, and in my memories, you continue to live. Today grant me the aspect of your spirit to connect to the love. I can choose to cherish this love to keep your spirit alive, or I can spiral into the turmoil of you not being here to distress your spirit. I have a choice as love being my healer or sadness being my destruction. Love is a way forward and my emotions are momentary". In strength and love, I carry myself forward through this dedication.

It doesn't matter how the clock ticks, how many breaths you take, the beholder of the key to THAT DOOR that opens, will only be at his beck and call. The battle of the living dead is neither here nor there. What is important that in this presence of time, LOVE your life, it is the most precious commodity, embrace it and live fully to your purpose, find your way through the depths of any challenges or darkness. Light always illuminates a path for those that believe in themselves. The power is within to overcome anything on your path. Life tests you through trails and tribulations to make you what you are today!

Painful changes are often an awakening to new beginnings and an awareness. It's also a purification of the soul, letting go, elimination of what was and is of no more. Along the way, focus on embracing the power of you, your divine wholesome blueprint of all that you are, and that precious soul before your incarnation on planet earth. No one is here to stay on this planet, we all return home one day. Take comfort in knowing that this too will pass, and you are going through what everyone experiences and goes through. Collectively every being, be it humans or animals, journeys through a painful experience of loss. This is the time to embrace, soak, nurture in self-love to heal.

It is through your toughest challenges you rise, through your weakest you become your strongest. Embrace and fight your way through, life is what you make of it! Not what life makes it for you.

Start today and wake up, open your heart, connect with your mind and soothe your soul. You are on your way to be in touch with yourself. The power of your light is the guiding force of any darkness that prevails. Believe in your OWN power, trust in your OWN guidance. Your life is in your control and not that of others. The greatest testament to you is LIVING, LEARNING, LOVING, LIFE. This is the essence of YOU, your lessons and experiences are a part of this human evolution. Recognise your true existence, to find peace.

PEACE

I AM, in embodiment and solace of peace in perfect equilibrium and balance

I choose this haven, for within this, is the sanctuary where I retrieve

To find myself outside of all storms and challenges of life

I am in control as I choose to be, amongst any chaos,

I strive to be in a state of being to overcome any obstacles.

My gain is more through peace and along comes joy & harmony

So it is, and so mote it be!

When you find peace, you are living life
When you find balance, you understand life
When you find gratitude, life enriches you with many blessings
Live each moment of life, you were given this for a purpose, waste not, want not, be fearless, be daring you will be surprised what a gift life really is!
That's the grace of living, to your will and free will!
Love who you are, and you are who you love! ©**KDhaliwal**

Chapter 9

CHOICES

Intentionally we have a way of sabotaging existing vibrational frequency without fully being conscious. Blocks are created for what we fear most and when all else fails we start questioning. The inner residing power needs to strengthen to ascend or normalize the frequency.

Sometimes when you are in the awareness of just being, all flows smoothly. However, in the essence of reality turmoil gathers and stews a pot of despair and ambiguity that shakes the flow and that core of just being.

This itself can become stifling to a point that anguish and despair become the main objective of questioning your choices. It is these choices that became your decisions to where you are today. Intensions originally set out may not conclude to the exact outcome that was envisioned.

It's not what or who you are, it's what you became through those choices and decisions you have made, to be who and what you are today. It doesn't really matter what circumstances were prevalent at that time, because ultimately always along this path of journey there are options or opportunities to change what does not suit any disposition. It's taking an inward inventory, to really understand the core of you of how and why you applied the choices made, which ultimately equates to the outcome. The blame game arises as it is always easier to blame situations, others, anything other than oneself.

A lifetime can easily pass, if one chooses not to be accountable for responsibility of one self. You are what you become, through your own choices. Our path becomes what we choose it to be. Change what you dislike, not what you fear. If you experience resistance, just be aware this will always often persist. Explore through your inward inventory of where this is coming from. Find a way that's going align in what, and how you want to feel, to match the action needed for a desired outcome.

It just needs small steady steps, and not a huge leap to achieve the thought process, to feel the heart resonance, and then align to link with the gut intuition. This should not be ignored; a gut is also a most important aspect of the amazing anatomy. This is also known as our second brain that communicates with the brain. The brain, the heart and the gut are intimately connected and play a huge role in the dynamics of the processes that occur consequently from choices made. A troubled intestine, or heart can send signals to the brain, just as a troubled brain can send signals to the gut and heart.

Emotions are felt in the gut. Feelings such sadness, anger, nervousness, fear, joy, and elation can be felt in the gut. The term "feeling sick to the stomach" describes a situation which involves mental or emotional anguish which can produce stress in the mind and the body. So as the saying goes if you're making a choice because of a gut intuition is often a reaction to an immediate situation. Anxiety, on the other hand, might be present regardless of its relevance to your current experience.

When you make a choice from your intuition, you may feel or you say things like, "I can't really explain it, but…" or "It just felt right" or, more likely, "It just felt wrong." "This isn't the right choice" If you get a strong and clear feeling that what you're doing isn't right, pay attention. ...

One of the easiest ways to tell the difference between a gut instinct and anxiety is by how long your symptoms last. If a choice is made from intuitive response, it's focus will be on the present, and the stance of awareness will feel neutral or calm. Choices made from anxious state will relate to the past and future, and carry a sense of dread and nervousness.

Thankfully the only choice that is not governed by you is, the one where you were placed in life, before you even incarnated on the earth planes. This where it could attain to be religion, faith, colour, caste etc. However, as you progress through life, the religion and faith can alter accordingly to your specific viewpoint or feelings as it arises. Importantly it should not matter or is relevant, other than the conditioning or programming one is endured to, through the stages in life.

What is relevant, life is for what you are today. Life is for living your purposes, experiencing your lessons, and overcoming your own challenges, as a part of your human evolvement. Life is not a comparison to another; we are all ONE. We all owe respect to each other. It should not matter what faith or religion you practice or you come from. No one is better or lower, all is equal. We ARE all ONE, yet as humans not as souls, we label ourselves as being proud of specific faith, religion, colour. Prior to our incarnation there were no labels. We collectively all come from one place and return to one place. No ONE individual is better than another, for better, for worse, for richer, for poorer, high-profile celebrity, low profile celebrity or plain ordinary joe blogs…we all collectively and equally go through one doorway, when the call from home comes… one home" accordingly as per our Creator/Source/God's law.

I stand proud of the life I was given, yes, I was conditioned into a belief system. As I was growing up, I knew deep in my heart this was not right. Many a times I fell out with my mother, specifically as a teenager when I was forced or coerced to go to a temple to seek the blessings of "God" etc. My argument or retaliation back to mum, would always be that I didn't need to go anywhere to find Source/God/divine, as my creator existed in my heart. It never went down well.

Long it continued into adult life, to the point at times I just gave in, and went just for having some peace. Thankfully only to the point I started making my own decisions to what felt right. I am grateful for all the lessons I was given, and fulfilled, and still learning to this day, as each one unfolds to a process of just being. I stand proud of who I am, not what I became, because neither am I a Sikh, Christian, Buddhist, Jewish, Hindu, Muslim etc etc. I AM just ONE, in the oneness and the presence of life. I am all that I am in the "I AM"

Today Declare: I AM, in control of me and not my emotions I have a choice today, I can either succumb, for what is momentary or take action, I am my thoughts, the power of my thoughts I control, and not my power controlled by others and incidences. I arise through each moment, come what may...I seize my day!

With the greatest of respect, I have no issues with religion or faith, history of others, because ultimately it is their own choice of what resonates with them individually. My perspective is that the awareness of all this historically, has arisen and been moulded from humans over time. I honour and respect you as an individual, if you disagree with this. The embodiment of all that you are is in this sacred heart of yours. We are all Source/God/Divine's creations, and once our lessons are completed on the earth school/plane, we return back to God/Source/Divine, not a religion or faith. Just one doorway for all, rich, poor, black, brown, white, royals, commoners etc...Just ONE doorway for ALL.

The pathway to happiness is the way to go from being the best person you can be without being a stranger to oneself. Once you have tamed the inner system and graduated to a level of being completely confident in being alone with your own thought system, you then become much more connected with being. More importantly you can feel a profound deeper connection between your inner self, emotions and feelings. This level reward system allows a golden opportunity for the whole of your existence to become the greatest joy you have created in this lifetime, it's an amazing achievement that takes progress to attain.

To achieve this level, you are able to overcome obstacles of the negative traits from the thought, feeling, emotion that would automatically initiate you to act from within whatever you were presented with and consequently make those choices.

Life is not what it is, but what you make of it. There is no fast way or slow way, just a pace to go from one day to the next. Along this process you start finding a new you, a real you under the surface of all the circumstances that you have been subjecting yourself to. I'm not going to elaborate the cliche about the layers of onions that are peeled before you get to the core. The core of you has always been there, just suppressed from the freedom of movement of free will of your own existence. The value of your freedom is your own personal choice, as is the power of the choice you select. Every decision from any choice is of the doing of what you deemed right for you, at that given time. It doesn't matter whether it was influenced or cohesive or what you thought was right or wrong. The outcome presented will be the predominant predictive effect of that.

The fact that one awakens to a dawning of the reality of life choices that have not been a favourable result, or outcome is the most significant aspect of a true identity of awareness of life itself. This can be seen as the most profound aspect of a person's existence in the present moment of their existence.

No one can like you, or love you as you do. The power of this recognition towards your self is honouring a validation that you are a lovable being. Think back the yonder years of being a joyful child, your parents loved, adored and protected you, throughout your upbringing. We all have to grow up, the love will always be there, but the joyous exuberance dissipates inwards, that inner child is still you. Life takes over and the inner child is forgotten.

Not everyone will have what another has, there will be some that didn't really have a loving childhood, or endured traumatic events and experiences. There is never a comparison but there will always be a difference between believing that you are a person of the highest potential in your own mind for your life, to not being able to see what others think about you in the same way that you do for yourself. If a childhood is sacrificed for whatever reasons or events into adulthood, then ultimately any choices made from those experiences will often lead to a lifetime of regrets.

Our inner child is the connection you have within yourself to your child self, and your childhood memories. This part of us can either make it or break it when it comes to facing situations in adulthood, because the reaction tendencies are often reflected as the behavioural patterns that we ingress to and act from. It holds emotions, memories and beliefs from the past that are wounds, which could be from those traumas, abuse, abandonment or unmet emotional needs.

If you're feeling frustrated or stuck in some aspect of your life, it's probable that your inner child is needing some attention. Stuck points in present day life, could be difficulties at work, in parenting, finding or keeping love, deepening relationships or setting boundaries. You may notice that you're experiencing fear, perfectionism, anxiety or are avoiding certain people, places or experiences. These are all ways that your inner child is attempting to feel safe. When the inner child is running the show, it'll choose behaviours, choices and thoughts based on unconscious beliefs or memories from the past, and based on what the inner self would need to feel safe.

Our Inner child is not aware of the reality of our adult self, because it is stuck way back there...in childhood. If this inner child lived with instability, uncertainty or danger, it will hold you back from making changes. You may notice a fearful part, afraid of you trying new things or moving forward.

So, what is the choice we have? It is giving you an awareness by allowing you an opportunity to reparent oneself, by addressing those unmet needs. It becomes a self-discovery journey to assist you to understand the behaviours, and to become aware of the emotional hurt and to become "unstuck" so that you can facilitate past those blockages, to cultivate the balance of creativity, flexibility, responsibility, connectivity and consistency. The merger between your adult self and your inner child self has to meet and get to know each other, to then heal from it, to embrace to a more authentic life for all hopes and dreams of the future.

Open up and tune in to learn about your inner child's needs, pains, hopes, and dreams, and taking steps to making them happen. Connect with your inner child, beginning a dialogue, and developing a relationship with it.

Infuse all the exhilaration of those feelings and memories of happiness and love into whatever experience you may be experiencing now. On the other side of this if you had an unhappy childhood, then think how you can be happier by being able to feel that happiness in your heart again in the moment of now. Give yourself the chance to acknowledge that you are worthy of much greater joy than your past. Change what is in your mind to make your future more meaningful and better than your past. Give, give and give to yourself. Love you like your life counted on it. Endorse your being of the worth that you are, because you matter. Don't forget who you are, and leave that vulnerable lost self of you alone in the past. Reconnect and release the innermost of yourself (inner child) that got lost in the abysmal depths of your subconscious body and mind. Allow what needs to flourish through now. Nothing is ever lost it's just that you forgot the little self, way back as the big life took hold.

Love is the epitome of all that you are, it's within you from the moment of your inception to the present and beyond. The soul of YOU is Love beyond measure, enjoy today from your soul without the attachment of it being anything less. You are worth more than what you validate yourself with! Honour yourself with gratitude. LOVE is the state of your whole being...feel and immerse in the presence of this energy, flow unconditionally and tap into the reservoirs you hold within; love is the creation of all that you are! Love is the nourishment for your soul, this divine nectar is the embodiment of all that you are. Love you, love life, what you make of it, is what you become. It starts with you, first and foremost, give to you that you deserve! This love fuels the energy of all the creation that you are. Embrace your love beautiful soul, for your guiding light is fuelled by LOVE. Love your existence, and you become who you love beautiful one.

INNERCHILD

I AM, a free spirit, roam wherever I may

I retrace my steps to the innocence of childhood, mind, body and spirit so free

No hassles, no thoughts, no worries, just tender love, playfulness and fun

This I invoke to escape the restrains of adulthood, to seek what got lost in transit of growing up, I am a loving being just tapping in to retrieve those feelings of joy and happiness.

So it is, and so mote it be!

Divine blessings to each and all, I honour and respect you. It is only through the choices we make we become. I may not like me some days, I may not like how the circumstances may have unfolded, but I am still me, and you know what, I love me for who I am, not just for today but for all the tomorrows, not just the past, but for all the future and beyond.

Recognition of your empowerment is by owning your power, don't give it away! Look where you are today, that itself is powerful. Journeying through life's highs and lows, each lesson learned, each challenge overcome is a testament of strength.

EMPOWERMENT

I AM, in control of my life choices and responsible for myself, I live my life in empowerment of ME. Your mind is a very powerful tool, utilise it! to its optimum, to achieve the maximum! Only you have the control over you, the rest just flows and follows, feel the empowerment of YOU....your path... your journey...your destiny...make it what you want...YOUR choice. Be the free spirit you are, and let go what holds you down!!! Shower your life full of many beautiful moments and blessings. Let go, move forward and release what no longer serves or is of any purpose; the path is already there; conquer your journey and embrace your efforts, it is those small steps that weave a wonderful tapestry of your life, allow it to catch your breath when you look back!

So it is, and so mote it be!

I want to end this chapter by offering you a gift of a deep cleansing, and connecting of your Inner Child Healing Meditation. Please honour yourself by retreating to a room where you won't be disturbed. You could lie on a bed, or sit on a couch, whatever is your choice. To create the perfect ambience in the room of your choice, it will assist to play some relaxing music, a scented candle (optional) you could record this, and listen to it, or have someone read the script to achieve the complete relaxing benefits.

Relaxation:

Get yourself in a comfortable position, lying or seated, in your mindset bring a sense of relaxation all around you. Close your eyes and take a deep breath and exhale, just let go of anything that does not need to be here. Just tune into your breath, allowing the mind and the physical to come into sync...now inhale...exhale... releasing any tension.

Become aware of the rise and fall of your chest, with each IN and OUT breath, just by concentrating on breathwork, will completely get you to a place of peacefulness. If any thoughts are rising in your mindset, just gently allow them to fade away, just focus on your breathing.

Now inhale a soulful breath of prana...the life force, and imagine allowing yourself to connect within, and gently exhale, feel the body letting go, releasing with each in, and out breathe of any stress, negativity that may have accumulated.

Breathe in LOVE...breathe out FEAR...breathe in HOPE... breathe out NEGATIVITY...feel the body succumbing to a state of peacefulness. Continue with the breathing until it starts becoming deep and shallow, deeper still, your whole vessel letting go.

I NOW INVOKE THE ANGELIC KINGDOM OF LIGHT to assist in this healing meditation.

Visualisation Journey:

Imagine a beautiful golden warm light above your head, as it enters it soothes your mind, allowing any thoughts that may still be there to dissipate, feel the warm glow travel to your face...neck...shoulders...relaxing all muscles...into the chest... the back...the glow encasing each muscle group with warmth, as it succumbs to release the tightness and tension...travelling to the pelvis...the buttocks...legs...to the soles of your feet. This warm golden light extends outwards...completely wrapping and cocooning you in light...this light now infuses into your heart centre...

You are NOW relaxed...in a peaceful state...breathing is very shallow...the whole of your vessel is caressed in this golden light, and feels eternally blissful...feel the body, the mind, and the heart in perfect alignment of one consciousness...oneness...complete utter centredness...reaching a place of our inner being... Now extend the light from your heart outwards in every direction, almost like you are radiating a ball of sunshine. This light is the ebb and flow of your life, and that precious soul of yours...allow the light from the sunshine to illuminate your path...to direct you to a way forward...lifting any and all darkness, shadows and sorrows.

Recognise the beautiful being you are...you have a purpose greater than you are aware of...don't allow the obstacles of fear...negativity...anxiety...anger...and so forth to entrap and engulf you away from the reality of your existence...you are on a path to fulfil your purpose...to learn your lessons...to gain your experiences...as a greater part of your evolution.

Now imagine holding yourself in your heart centre...this space is the source of unconditional love that supports and nourishes the whole of your being...get a sense of that love and immerse with it...this unconditional love is supporting and powerfully healing...silently invoke to yourself...I AM LOVE...I AM HAPPY...I AM WORTHY...I AM WELL...I AM HAPPY...drop any resistance you feel...any reasons why you should not be loving...not be happy...not be well, and any feelings of not being worthy of happiness and health...allow the light in the heart to expand deeper and deeper...cleansing any residue that does not serve a purpose...your love is your healing...love is the divine nectar...through your heart you are one with the universe...there is no separation between you and what is outside of you…as you love yourself so shall the universe reciprocate that love to nourish and enrich you.

Silently invoke MY VESSEL IS MY TEMPLE…MY BREATH IS MY PRANA…LIFE FORCE…MY MIND IS TRANQIL AND CALM…MY HEART IS LOVING…I AM PURE LOVE…I AM A BEING HEALED BY LOVE. Your life is a gift, treasure and cherish yourself, always in every way…love is the language of the universe…love is the flame of divinity and LOVE is the greatest healer.

Now imagine the younger you in the heart…call out your name with love and in tenderness…establish a connection with the younger you by expressing how much you love them…and ask for FORGIVNESS…please forgive me…for the hurt and pain I may have caused you…through my words and actions…forgive me for forgetting you and leaving you…I am here for you…I love you and I will protect you…

Your mind may confront of many reasons why you are not worthy of being forgiven…just acknowledge this and let go of the memories and any resistance in you to your inner child… just continue with the forgiveness…breathe out any resistance… and breathe in forgiveness…feel the forgiveness throughout your whole being, releasing the toxicity from your energy system… freeing you…let go of fear, anger, misery, heartache, sadness and any pain…repeating Forgive me, I love you 3times.

Feel you heart becoming lighter…your inner child smiling, uplifting your whole essence of your being, as all negative emotions are cleansed and eliminated. The light within your soul is shining like a diamond as you and your inner child merge and make peace. Reconnect and let the love and the immense light radiate intertwining both into oneness, bathe in the unconditional love and the showers of blessings…you are healed...you are at peace...you are safe...you are loved...nurtured and protected as thy will all falls into place...in oneness...in this beautiful temple within your physical...resonate and bask in this peaceful sensation...why look elsewhere when all is within reach...access this for your whole being on all 4 levels...your physical body...emotional body...mental body and your spiritual body...now slowly bringing yourself back to the presence of the here and now...TAKE A DEEP BREATH...as you return to the external environment...EXHALE...feel the difference...you will be completely at ease to when you commenced this meditation... let the joy in your heart greet your world...you owe it to yourself and your inner child...you are worth it...May the Universe shower you endlessly with a magnitude of blessings...YOU DESERVE IT!

Chapter 10

OPULENCE PROGRAM

PURPOSE

I AM, living my soul mission and purpose of my life-plan journey. The purpose of you, me and all, is simply to enjoy and just be in those precious moments. The journey of life will always present challenges, these are the lessons that evoke us for growth, why waste time creating blocks that hinder your path...you are a precious soul travelling through the earth planes, come what may. The purpose of your life is to fulfil your mission, so your soul feels complete. Define the depths of YOU and your purpose, and all will unfold as it needs to. Who said human evolvement was anything but easy...applaud yourself for the many challenges you have faced to where you are today, these very life experiences and lessons are the moulding of you! If you have not defined the purpose of YOU yet, just know that you are serving the purpose of YOUR life plan! after all you are the story of your life...let it be a bestseller...

So it is, and so mote it be!

How would you personally classify your SELF. Upper class, lower class, 1st class, 2nd class, superior or inferior? these categories your own self-worth. Do you recognise your self-worth? What can be more magnificent and opulent than thyself, you are your best being and much more. The word opulence itself means grandeur, lavish, abundance, and splendour. In a nutshell the very best version of your better elite self!

Do you like or love yourself, that itself will say a lot about you. Self- love begins with you, love thyself, first and foremost, this alone is more than ample power of all that you are on this magnificent journey, this realisation of your self -worth, is beyond immeasurable, all is within, tap into what, and who you are. Believe in the creation of YOU and your purpose, love yourself above and beyond any flaws. Love is the key, and you are the beholder of this, unlock this potential and witness the glory of all that you are, feel the root and the essence of your being on this planet earth, the vibration changes to a whole new level. You are the stance in your being. Realise how unique you truly are, you are an amazing being, enjoy this essence of YOU! You are a vessel of love, the embodiment of wholesome and wholeness.

The Opulence Program was developed to discover YOU in this mighty "I AM" We are not just a physical vessel. We consist of an energetic system known as the 4-body system, which is broken down into The Physical Body; The Mental Body; The Emotional Body and The Spiritual Body. (Previously mentioned in Chapter 3 through the PEMS system)

Each of these energetics comes into play in accordance of how we feel, how we perceive, how we react and how we deliver in accordance to what is presented in any given situation of our being. It assists you to progress your way forward positively for personal growth and development. At the same time, it also aims to deliver a unique message of actions/choices that conveys the behaviour or belief.

The aim of this program defines "Who you are" and to predominately become aware how you act, react, feel, become and be free.

I do hope you enjoy utilising this program for fun or to facilitate your way through life and situations, and importantly stimulate a change from a stance that is not working with your persona and energy. The array of selection offered can be diversified to fit with something specific to you and personalised.

So, let's start by asking "Who Are You?" not everyone can answer this quickly. Most will pause, think, and hesitate, some will struggle. Only you know you better than anyone else, yet to define yourself, there will be an obstacle of some sort through hesitation.

If on the other hand, you were asked "Are you Happy, Positive, Vibrant and accepting of life?" "Or is there something missing?" There will no doubt be a hesitation here to answer.

If you were given the opportunity to make tangible changes or modify, perhaps even to adapt, to fully receive the gratification and rewards, you would be curious.

Life itself is curious because we are consistently learning. Life is not about hesitations or long pauses; it's about being in the presence of the moments that create a fulfilling way forward. Any programming from childhood, and comfort zones are mere stumbling blocks, these blocks are a stationery point. It just allows us to stop, a stop point will be a choice point, which is a sign to become aware, and to go on to change something, so the flow can either continue in a progressive way, or if you continue plodding away as you are, then this becomes a destructive way.

Just to give you a few examples: Traffic jams or blocks will either make you stop or divert. This also applies to your life journey, you can either stay where you are, or move and progress to where you need to be. Another example: Blockages of a drain anywhere in your house/building or even outside will have consequences- it will either cause a build-up, or burst scenario, it's impediment to unblock so the system works, and flows efficiently and smoothly. Therefore, life too should not become stationery, because a block impedes the flow. It is up to you to unblock or find a way round it.

Life isn't just about how it flows; it revolves around planning too. We plan when we are cooking, meeting friends or family, doing shopping, planning for the weekend or social events etc. By planning you are already on your way to do, and to achieve that specific task, we know what we want, where and when we want it to be. As the saying goes:

"If you fail to plan, you plan to fail" quote by Benjamin Franklin

Recognise the exuberance of your own life on a grandeur level of being. You are a magnificent soul habituating a physical form. Let this light shine like a diamond, because you are a pure gem!

Optimise Personal power, Uplifting Life Effortlessly, Nurturing Challenging Experiences = **OPULENCE**

Optimise – make the best use within current or present constraints of life, thereby improving to reach a much higher level of performance.

Personal power – being a positive impact to one self, and an inspiration to others. Personal power comes from having self-awareness, confidence, and the ability to draw others in with your charisma or wisdom through your positive and state of mind. Thoughts - create your life, Feelings - affect our thinking, Behaviour -Our behaviour dictates our results in life, Focus – decides where your energy flows.

Uplifting- to rise above and to elevate oneself, feeling motivated through inspiration, which offers encouragement to boost yourself through any challenging circumstances. Uplifting yourself through realigning your thoughts. Staying focused and connected, more importantly being kind to oneself.

Motivating someone else encourages you too. It gives you a feeling of positivity and makes you feel like you've made a difference in someone else's life. If you're uplifted, you're feeling exhilarated, buoyed up with good spirits.

Life – You are your life, a being here to live a purpose, with a purpose to fulfil. Your lessons will be the experiences and the making of who you become. The human spirit includes our intellect, emotions, fears, passions, and creativity. The human spirit is considered to be the mental functions of awareness, insight, understanding, judgement and other reasoning powers.

Effortlessly - transcending the need for physical action, just simply allowing what needs to unfold as things happen, without fear. Just having faith and trust, having compassion to allow oneself to be spiritually aligned with true source energy, with ease, without expectation to then radiate joy, and wisely and intelligently making use of what is already available, and to gracefully, respectfully, and gratefully accept whatever comes to you as a gift from the universe. Being aware of your physical stance through your body language. Our beautiful physical vessel is a part of the 4-body system - P= physical, E=emotional, M= mental and S= spiritual. It all interconnects together.

Nurturing- Self-care, self-love towards oneself. Caring and prioritising your needs first and foremost, above and beyond anything else. Being fully present, validating your feelings, acknowledging all positive traits of oneself, being kind to oneself, to balance the physical with that of the mindset.

Challenging - Facing challenges and navigating one's way through life. Obstacles in life are presented as challenges to either overcome them, to learn from the struggles, and grow and evolve, because they are an important facet of our development, it builds our resilience capacity, and lays a solid foundation for success in later life. The challenges are our lessons that we have to experience, in a way it tests our ability and determination. It also stimulates growth through bad times.

Experiences- No one can live life without learning something. What you learn and experience can often determine your success or failure in life. Effortful learning combined with real life on the job experience is a winning formula for success. Your choices and your experiences help create the person that you are. Each experience and knowledge gained through living; create the person you are today. How much you like yourself is also directly influenced by your goals.

Every thought will create emotions and feelings to evoke your body to act to those projections of choices made. Make a concerted effort of always choosing to embrace the beauty of all that is within by aligning a positive choice by taking control to overcome whatever maybe wearing you down, in that moment. A moment can either become radiant or dull. Allow yourself to bloom by energising and showering your thoughtform by injecting love to create a powerful dose of positivity.

Just like as a new day rises, come what may, rain or shine, wind or snow, every image evokes a reaction. Let it be a smile in your soul & heart, innocence, fun, free, contentment and beauty. There is beauty in everything, and just sometimes it's just allowing your heart to smile, to feel free from the debris and clutter of adulthood life! Life is full of magical moments.

Today Declare: *I have a choice to either rise above the feeling that is evoked from an emotion and flow with it, or be controlled and succumb to the pool of doom, depravity and darkness. Trust, faith and love conquers all, but above all peace is my inner strength. May today and all my days bring me endless blessings, happiness and peace always in loving gratitude, may the flame of the divine alight my heart, the joy of life allows my spirit to dance, my soul to be illuminated in radiance of continuous eternal light and love. I embrace the glory of today, I make time to refuel and nurture my soul, thankful for what has been, and grateful for what has yet to come. I am responsible for the choices = outcome.*

Are you ready to experience OPULENCE and overcome any challenges that may presently be hindering any progress. Recognise the powerful being that you are in a grandeur way and facilitate your way through life by applying PEMS from an opulence perspective. This can be done in any order that you desire, there is no right or wrong way.

From your <u>Physical</u> Body (Body Language) **Own** your **P**ower, passionately for personal growth, **Unconditionally** without pressure, **L**earning and evolving, **E**mpowering oneself, **N**ourishing your wholesome and wholeness, **C**onsistently, **E**mbracing your accomplishments. (**OPULENCE**)

PHYSICAL BODY	THOUGHT	BEHAVIOUR	EMOTIONS & FEELINGS
Own your Power	self esteem	Positive	happiness, contentment
Passionately for personal growth	self confidence	feeling good about oneself	motivated, inspired, elated
Unconditionally without pressure	self-love	acceptance, manageable, steady steps towards goals	being kind to yourself, feeling good about self, grounded and centered
Learning and evolving	self-assured	acknowledging any mistakes are a learning curve, to pick oneself up and go on	belonging, pride, love, affectionate, acceptance and strength
Empowering oneself	self-belief	making a conscious decision to take charge of your destiny, making positive choices, taking action, being confident in your ability to make and execute decisions.	Positive mental attitude, encouragement, motivated and boost of self, Assertive. Sense of control and purpose in life.
Nourishing your wholesome and wholeness	endorsing self	recognition, standards, experiences	appreciated, safe, stability, accomplished
Consistently	every moment	uplifted, morale	triumph, satisfaction
Embracing your accomplishments	achievements	being thankful, in gratitude, compassion, pride	success, recognition and rewards

From your <u>Emotional</u> Body (Feelings) – Open hearted, Positively, Utilise, Love, Energetically, Nurture within to Calmness and centredness and be Empathetic towards oneself. (OPULENCE)

EMOTIONAL BODY	THOUGHT	BEHAVIOUR	EMOTIONS & FEELINGS
Open Hearted	aligned, forgive, heal and feel	resistance to any bitterness, helpful, kind, honest and generous	receptive, expansive, forgiving, peaceful and relaxed
Positively	achievements	happiness, elated,	joy, hope, inspiration, satisfaction, contentment
Utilise	practical, effective	adaptive, applying skills,	action-active, motivated
Love	appreciation, high regard, wellbeing and happiness, satisfied	trust, pleasure, commitment	joy, happiness, excitement, intimate, euphoria, affectionate
Energetically	reactivated, re boosted, revitalised, recharged	positively energised, energy in motion & movement	desire and focus to accomplish each goal/task, vibrational frequency
Nurture within	endorsing self, validation, growth, development	supporting, encouraging, engaging	feel good factor, joy, love, compassion, empathy, peace, acts of service
Calmness and Centredness	presence of peace, relaxation, patience and ease	grounded and focused, in control	equanimity, balanced, aligned, gratitude, logical, clarity of mind, soothing, awareness, breathing, breath,
Empathetic	self-fulfilled, valued, safe, caring, loving	sense, understand, point of view,	kindness, fulfilment, non-judgemental. Communication, compassionate

From your <u>Mental</u> Body (Thoughts) – Open minded to Possibilities, Uplifting through inspiration and Liberating oneself by Educating the mind with New positive thought patterns, and de-cluttering negative programmes Consciously to encourage Empowerment. (OPULENCE)

MENTAL BODY	THOUGHT	BEHAVIOUR	EMOTIONS & FEELINGS
Open minded	welcoming and willing to consider new ideas	willing to learn, explore, acknowledge and explore different ideas perspectives, and concepts	thinking rationally, equally, being calm and empathetic, humble and respectful
Possibilities	chances, probability, achieving, feasibility	motivation and desire to achieve scope of goals	being hopeful, committed, sense of satisfaction, empowered, inner strength, optimistic
Uplifting	improving, openness to change, inspired, boosted, excited	positive attitude, being present, an inspiration	happiness, empowered, contentment, kindness
Liberating	emancipated, free, non-judgemental	freewill, determination, free choice	elation, freedom, centred, grounded, free, positive, confident
Educating	learning, exchanging knowledge/ experience, problem solving, solutions, decision making	cognitive awareness of situations and stimulus, guidance,	growth, evolvement, progression, calm, nurturing, options, interest
New	learning and adapting to something new, ideas, knowledge and experiences	learning and experiencing new habits, new changes	curiosity, fearless, empowering, elevating
Calmly	peace, ease, sereneness, tranquil, harmonious	gentle, kind, empathic, sensitive, level headed	compassionate, free from agitation and anxiety, relaxed, amicable, approachable
Empowerment	self-control, motivation, confidence, equality	safe, self-efficient, stability and security	self-esteem, fearless, powerful, strong, strength, grounded, centered, aligned

From your <u>Spiritual</u> Body – (Higher self) **O**neness in **P**erfect alignment of soul, body and mind, **Universally** connected through **L**ove that is the epitome of an **E**nlightened being, **N**avigating **e**arthly life, and rooted through higher self of **C**onsciousness for **E**volvement **(OPULENCE)**

SPIRITUAL BODY	THOUGHT	BEHAVIOUR	EMOTIONS & FEELINGS
Oneness	unified, whole, state of being	closeness, affinity, union, connection, peaceful, acceptance of being	interconnectedness, transcendence, inherent goodness, open hearted, peaceful mind
Perfect	faultless, flawless	balanced, perfectionist, self-worth	forgiving, positive, selfless, caring, empathetic,
Universally	everywhere, whole, entire, something greater, infinite	trust, faith, compassionate,	cosmic, whole, contentment, awe, vastness
Love	connection, in awe, honouring, valuing, adoration, admiration	unconditional, non-judgemental, non-critical, pureness, kindness, joyful, helpful, graceful, grateful, respectful	forgiving, loving, gratitude, selfless, selflessness caring, empathetic, happiness, euphoria
Epitome	perfect example of something,	strong, strength, empowered, motivating	values and wisdom, embodying, statement
Navigating	moving from one point to the next, directing, to lead, route planning	in control, methodical, strategizing, evaluating	taking action, planning & flowing in positive trajectory, moving forwards, finding your way through diversions & pitfalls to reach where you need to be.
Consciousness	Awareness, presence, state of oneness	deepening connections, compassionate, empathetic, inter connectedness	transcendent state, love, peacefulness, just being, compassion, divine
Evolving	higher evolution, growth & development	practising self-care, optimistic and positive, deeper connections,	heightened intuition, sensitivity, at ease, peaceful state of being, helpful, kind,

Life is a mystery that can become a mastery when you attain a way of living to the desired expectation of your own values, to be where you want to be, and not where you are in this moment in this stance. The mystery of life is attempting to solve it, but when you connect to a realisation of the purpose of life, the flow of your journey and your path to a living, you truly awaken. It is at this point you have mastered your life to a way of being. We are all on a spectacular journey on the earth planes, attempt to living life, value and enjoy each sacred moment. A moment will come and go but the memory of this will be etched for a lifetime. Welcome the abundance of cosmic blessings into this greatest mystery... LIFE....Living it, breathing it, flowing it, and unfolding it to a beautiful revelation of your human existence! You are worth it more than you give yourself credibility. The highest accolade of appreciation is You of yourself. If you struggle to understand and define the essence of you in this great mystery, how can you expect another to resolve this for you.

Precious moments, hours, days, weeks and then years are trivialised for what? Time just surpasses for regrets, thinking becomes arduous, and actions become re-lapses. The awareness of the presence becomes powerful, gone what has, what needs to come is in your control from this moment. Encapsulate your presence...NOW. Observe and allow the journey of your life transform into an opulent way of living.

ENERGY

I AM, a consistent connection in the ebb and flow of Life. I am only disconnected if I am not basking in the glorious energy frequency. This potent energy of the Universe is the powerhouse of creation that births intentions, from thoughts & choices into fruition. This super power is a gift of manifestations of all our hearts desires. Energy aligns with energy with a perfect connection that creates the wavelength of this awesome vibrancy, all is as is, in perfect alignment & harmony. You are the power; you are your thoughts and choices but above and beyond you are a being of energy. It is all about the intention, strive forward to achieve your goals...only YOU can do it...tap within your resources...your power...your energy. Only you will make it what it will become. What you think is what you create, your mind is a powerful tool & transmitter. Your thoughts are always transmitted on the Universal frequency, a cosmic wavelength; a powerful frequency that is consistently ON....allow the song of the Universe to merge with your thoughts and create a beautiful symphony of your life, connect to the creation of your chorus.

So it is, and so mote it be!

LOVE WHO YOU ARE

AND YOU ARE WHO YOU LOVE!

THE INFINITE OPULENT SOUL

CHAPTER 11

GRATITUDE

TODAY

I AM, in gratitude for today and the blessings it unfolds. The morning dawn is greeted beautifully by the birds as they sing the chorus of another new day. Arise to embrace the day, as it ends reflect with happiness in your heart, mind and the soul. Yesterday's battles are of the past, today you have control, the future is another day, today choose to stand tall, any challenges that arise are only obstacles to get through and overcome. You can either choose to be defeated or be empowered.

So it is, and so mote it be!

Thank you is a tiny echo of a huge impression of gratitude. It's an acknowledgement of appreciation. Do you appreciate who you are? And where you are or stand today? Even the tiniest good can be overlooked by havoc amidst any crisis one may be going through. This is a two-way process, it's not all about oneself, it can also be rendered towards another, to make a difference to them, that you may not be aware of. Just a smile can lift, and leave a lasting impression on another if they are going through a bad day. A hello, hi, good day, or good morning doesn't cost anything but is such a rewarding impression on another.

You are not the only one surviving every day, come what may. Another maybe worse or even less off, a small gesture can get one through. Always be and, become in awareness at all times of you and others.

Today Declare: *I am in charge from this moment, this stance, I am powerfully equipped to overcome at my free will. Replenishment for the soul is what I give it! You are in control, have an amazing day full of sweet melodies, recount every moment as wonderful blessings, in all that has unfolded, for each is a lesson for our growth & evolvement. May today and all your days be blessed and good, it starts and ends with you, make it count!*

It is through our toughest challenges we arise, where there were blessings in our amidst, we are in denial of recognising any examples of good times. We tend to suppress the good times and focus awareness on bad times, and not on the lessons that were for the making of us. In life everything is a balance, we cannot have happiness without sadness, tears without joy, darkness without light, the sun without the moon, the warmth without the cold, hunger without food and so forth. Source/Creator God, made opposites and equality in everything. Male/female, left / right...etc etc.

The route, the path of our life becomes a destination, we are on a journey. It has a start –a beginning, and it has to finish – an ending. The journey will never be smooth, there will be diversions, there will be problems, the ups and downs throughout the route will be our battles, these are our challenges to overcome to make each of us stronger and become who we are today. These experiences are life lessons that make us who we become. Never underestimate the powerful being that you are and always be in recognition of your journey, because that is your journey, not another's.

Sometimes it's not about how your life journey is actually flowing, but how you are merging within this flow to reach where you need to be effortlessly, without constraints and blockages, that you inevitably created through fear. When we are all jolly i.e. happier times, we just relish, and enjoy it without any acknowledgement or gratitude. If on the opposite of this, we are submerged through the bad times, we collectively focus energies on the negatives of everything in that moment or time. This is a time to reflect in that moment, it is through these bad times, that we are moulded and strengthened, therefore we should be open, and be aware of these lessons and pitfalls. We are not concerned when all is good, regretfully when anything is all but good, we think the worst, maybe that song **by Billy Ocean "when the going gets tough, the tough get going"** will steer you towards helping yourself in grace, and with gratitude, you are after all important to you, and this quote
by Michel De Montaigne

"He who fears he will suffer, already suffers because he fears."

will at least evoke you into awareness there can only be good even from destruction**.**

Never focus on the lack because you attract more of it, be in gratitude by amplifying the positive from a negative situation. Love instead of hatred, richness instead of poverty, happiness instead of sadness, joy instead of tears. More instead of less and so forth. Be intoxicated with gratitude, fuel it with love because the rewards of this simple acknowledgment magnifies ten folds to deliver the positive affect. It truly doesn't matter if you don't see it, just feel it, and you will receive it immediately because its effect is already in the dynamics of the universal energy.

More importantly ask each time, what is it teaching me, what have I, or can I learn from this experience? We all endure certain storms in our lives, but we also need to be thankful because we arise from those situations. It may not be immediate but over time we have a dawning, a realisation. Certainly, to a point of awakening or awareness that we don't repeat or put ourselves in that repetitive cycle again.

Take a leap of faith, believe in yourself and trust the process, you are the power to your mindset, and you can adapt the patterns of behaviours to achieve the desired results. What you plant in your mind- ie seeds is what comes into fruition. So be aware of those thoughts!

It's in the depthless of your inner being to fulfil and interject love and empathy for a situation in midst of any dilemma or crisis, take time to just stand back, breathe and understand without judgement or criticism. Your overview or opinion is not that of whatever you are faced with. One has to deal with what's in front or ahead with compassion to obtain the desired effect or result.

It is only then you can step back and acknowledge it wasn't as difficult as you perceived it in your mindset, but the outcome of the effect was surprisingly far better than what may have been or was anticipated.

Learning to let go and, not rise to anything, is an astonishingly strong skill, eventually with practice you have found a way of dealing with it, and there comes a point where it will no longer bother you, in ways that it did previously.

We allow ourselves to be consumed in situations unnecessarily, due to the circus of thoughts that entertain the mind. Only you have the power to rein those thoughts in and tame them! They can run riot, but only you are responsible for controlling them. You need to dig deep to find your own strength to release any of these negative thoughts, and any limiting beliefs that have been weighing you down and staunching your evolution. These unhealthy patterns of behaviour are not serving a purpose for your soul growth and development. Do you want to progress on your journey or hinder your path, only you can determine where you want to be, stuck or moving forward? Everything changes the moment you change your perception. You are capable of achieving whatever you put your mind to, as long as you are willing to work and navigate towards your desired goal.

Take for example if you're driving a car, you wouldn't necessarily drive on the wrong side or over a cliff, because you are aware of the dangers, even if you don't drive, you wouldn't just simply put yourself in the middle of a dangerous situation, because you are aware of the implications, yet many of us are in a slumber when it comes to manoeuvring our life in the direction of our hopes, dreams and goals. Somehow, we just don't step into awareness of the presence to go forth.

A building is built on firm foundations so it doesn't collapse, the same goes for your own stature and stance of life and being, build firm foundations by aligning your thoughts, towards personal development. Focus all your energy to fulfil the desired reality than allowing any emotions to rule the mindset, the playground. The playground can be a happy place or a bad place. Only through choice and perseverance you have the courage and determination towards the real you to overcome any obstacles.

Take inventory of your Life trajectory: be in gratitude of your mighty self and being! Acknowledge and validate the beautiful soul you are by affirming you are worthy, you are someone, and that you are a powerful beautiful being that has a lot to offer. This is not difficult to do, the greatest validation one can give to themselves is to honour themselves first and foremost, and everything else just follows. Why is it so difficult, to oneself? Yet, when anyone attends a Job interview- you sell yourself to best version of yourself and your abilities to get the job, yet when it comes to personal life flow, there are excuses of this, that, and everything. Take inventory of your life, change, amend, alter what you don't like, sitting on your laurels isn't going to make it happen. Everything takes action from learning something to achieving something. Learning to drive, swim, cook, walk, new language etc etc, so why make it so difficult to learn to see the real you!

Sometimes or maybe all the times, many of us forget to salute and thank our physical and its performance, we take our bodies for granted. If anything, this magnificent functioning system is always overlooked. One morning as I awoke, my body was extremely exhausted from the previous day, overdoing so many tasks. Instead of the deep sleep I had anticipated, I had endured the opposite, it was a restless night. I guess it was more to do with a funeral I had to attend of a dearest close friend. Again, from a spiritual mindset I understand that life is not an ending but a beginning in eternity, free from the shackles of human restraints, lessons and experiences and more importantly a mission completed. Yet the tenacity of the human self-level, submerges into the can of emotions from the grief. For me personally, I was going to be back at the same crematorium that my dearest beloved mum went to, so the wound of memories and emotions would no doubt surface through. It's only been 7months, so I am still going through the healing phases. For me I still have the comparison of the memories from "this time last year"

Nevertheless, I need to be gentle and kind to myself, and honour what comes up, to acknowledge, to release and heal, more importantly thankful for the experiences of a loving friendship and the memories. Not to hold on, but to let go of what no longer serves. The injustice to myself is to impede my peace and happiness. Those that leave us are finally free, yet we on a human level submerge ourselves through our own doing, into a deepest depth of sorrow. Those beings towards the end phase of their life journey, drop any resistance, and somehow come into a level of letting go, an inner knowingness not to fight the inevitable anymore. An awareness of a completion from a higher self-steps in. It could also be that the body just cannot cope or function to a level it once did, through such weariness it starts to give up. Some will have a strong mindset, (like my parents) yet at some point, the mind at some point, also has to drop into that sync of the body, and then to align with the heart in resonance of slowing the pace in all the systems of the body in preparation for soul extraction. The frequency and vibration of energy starts slowing into consciousness of peaceful state of being....SLOW is the process, slowing down. The energy system retracts back to reserve for the process of extraction. The fuel system starts slowing and shutting down. The consumption of food and drink no longer is needed for sustenance, the digestive system cannot perform like it did, all the signal system to all functions of the body is directed to SLOW down...breathing, moving, talking, keeping eyes open. Everything aligning to a peaceful state of consciousness. The only thing on this level, will be the hearing, which is still intact and heightened to hearing everything ie whispers, and possibly a touch from a loved one.

Our vehicle, our physical is a remarkable and highly intelligent system. Have anyone of us just paused to respect, honour this throughout living, NO, would most likely be the answer because it's taken for granted. Be in gratitude of your being, because it's functioning, and rendering a highest service to your vessel, a full operational system. Yes, there will be defects too ie (illness essence, mobility essence, mental essence etc) but importantly the vessel is still functioning until your last breath.

Kim Dhaliwal

My mantra:

"Thank you, my energy system. I am so grateful for all the hard work. I acknowledge you operate to highest optimum levels for the functioning of this vessel in pristine order. I am in deepest gratitude for my living, breathing and functioning of my state of wellbeing, all is perfectly aligned. Thank you for this reservoir of energy, the sustenance of my existence"

and so mote it be!

Never underestimate the power within. This powerful intelligence will always function. How you operate it, will be from the reins of your control. The power box is your mindset, how you control this will be the orchestrated patterns, behaviours from thoughts that fuel it.

GRATITUDE

I AM, thankful for living a life of gratitude. Thank you, Universe! I thank each and every soul for being a part of my journey, for without you what purpose would I be fulfilling. A magical auspicious story can only be weaved with the connections. Each unique path will always continue and flow albeit with various diversions. Along the way it will also present you with opportunities to continue in equilibrium and balance. Always in gratitude to the Universe for all my lessons and blessings. May each and every beautiful soul, be endowed with a multitude of endless blessings and miracles. Acknowledge the Universe and it reciprocates back in rewards. Living a life of gratitude opens doors to the magic that flows miraculously 'Thank you Universe' for every experience and lessons learned!

So it is, and so mote it be!

Conclusion

The huge shift: what does it mean: Are you ready for this transformative energy and transgression. It's time to finally let go and transgress to the platform that awaits. It does feel like a beginning, a new life, releasing the old which is encumbersant of the past.

Feel the power, you are this powerhouse of your being, you are not the level attainment of that of a learner, your apprenticeship of life is long over, it's time to experience the elevated you. How you value yourself will be the importance of the role you play in your own life. Don't underestimate the powers within, there is so much more to you, than all the less you portray. The dejection is immersive. You are in this mass playground, but what are you enjoying, the joy is stripped away. All the tools are there, yet if not utilised, how can you expect a solid foundation of stance. Just like a building, it needs a solid foundation for the structure to be held in place, the various tools to utilise to formulate something to make an impression, a statement, and mainly a purpose or intent for why it was built, and for what purpose it will be utilised for. The same principles apply for one's being, yet the fulfilment of the joyful experiences of life and living becomes a stagnation of living. Life can decay away from all the conditioning and programmes, the preservation is to let go of the societal demands and constraints, free yourself to be the free joyful spirit. The structures are already crumbling away, because we have become what we supposedly are not to be, through conditioning. Become aware of who you are, ask yourself are you happy, wholesome and content with who you are, or is it time to focus on remedying this version of you, to the magnificent being that thrives life eloquently.

It's not about what makes sense or not, that itself doesn't matter. What should matter is who are you? What is the meaning of your life? Are you living it? A building has a value to show its worth for whatever specific or intent it was utilised for. What is the perspective of your value of you? Your statement should be invaluable, yet this will be difficult for most, as this shows that your worth of you is undervalued as you have no self-recognition of you, your stance and being. You are far far more than that.

For example, we sell ourselves at job interviews for a role and a salary that meets the expectations of your worthy of this (skills & experiences) relevant to the post. Why then is there a lack to life value of you to you, on one to one?

The dynamic energies shift from a slumbering experience to an immersive awakened experience. Let's consider the word LIVE…. exposes a VEIL…from the same letters, but when spelt backwards it reveals EVIL, and again the same letters expose VILE…

So, one should be living not subject only to live…in an awareness it becomes a different meaning. Let's take an example of "Live for every moment" sounds good, sounds perfect, sounds positive, sounds apt to apply. Now the same example but the live spelt backwards "Evil for every moment" straightaway it brings undesirable feelings and notions.

Therefore, living life should exactly be just that. "Living and loving life" "Live Life, love life" whereas the latter becomes "Evil life, love life" where's the joy in living that statement.

Wake up and be alive to living not just to live. Change your perceptions of what your reality and trajectories are in this moment…NOW and you have WON….always in the presence, if you are far from this, then you are defeated from within. The power is always in the presence of each moment…NOW and spell this backwards and you have WON, in that moment you are in control.

When we prioritize self-care, we are able to cleanse and balance our energy field, release negative emotions and thoughts, strengthen our connection to our higher self and source, and become more centered, grounded, and aligned with our purpose.

This wake up is your call!

LIBERATION

I AM, a free spirit, I surrender and release what no longer serves, I set myself free from any limitations, as I step forward to embrace the new awakening and reality. This is my liberation & freedom, I gracefully move forward in the cycle of life, the constant stream of the ups and downs, of giving & receiving. I arise like a Phoenix from any turbulence. I birth the new reality of all that will be, and so it is. Loving life always, in gratitude, I am thankful and grateful for even the smallest things provide huge dividends!

So it is, and so mote it be!

Final Word From Me To You

YOU ARE THE STAR!

I AM, the movie star of my life story, the reality of my magnificence and the awesomeness are magical. Honour yourself in all the glory that you are…recognise the mighty worth of YOU in your true alignment of your creation… know who you are and not what you are….don't rush your walk on this beautiful journey, pause and enjoy the moments that imprint not just a memory, but continuous lifetime treasures, make it rare one's in this vast Universe! Feel the joy within and illuminate the eternal light…open your eyes and fulfil your plan, life is a treasure…YOU… alone are the force of your own being…your flow…your thoughts…living it and make it count! One day, when this journey is complete, you will be in front of one almighty audience….make it a good flashback! The accolade for a good human being is a prestigious award presented by God.

So it is, and so mote it be!

Always remember that this life is precious, and each of us are on our own individual journeys. Lessons, experiences and challenges makes us what we are, if not stronger at least a bit wiser. You are only responsible for who you are and yourself only! Never allow anyone or anything to affect you, your choices or your decisions. If anyone makes you feel not so great about you, your life, or choices, it is nothing to do with you but a reflection of the other person. We have a powerful mind, and our thoughts create a story, which creates a feeling then an emotion. Anything we put in our mindset we are responsible for creating the havoc, be it anger, resentment, insecurity, failure, anxiety, all because we create the fear for cause and effect, therefore we become our own saboteurs of misery instead of living a life of joy, peace and happiness. Each of us are weaving a tapestry of our life, let it be a breathtakingly beautiful story! Life will always have ups and downs, a journey is a destination with diversions here and there, come what may, allow yourself to enjoy the ride! For when the day comes when we are called back home to God, we present him the tapestry for the life he gave us. Always in gratitude and love, for this is what and how our souls evolve, and that is what LIFE truly is!

FOOTPRINTS

I AM, the storyteller of my life, for every step leaves an imprint, footprints are the story that weave a tapestry, the journey of life. Whatever the disruption, diversion, the destination, the flow of endings and beginnings, make every step count. For each and every lesson and experience that has moulded you in preparation for the next chapter "life is a gift! and each one of us is a miraculous creation of LOVE!" Love you, love your existence. The imprint you leave is the tapestry you created...make it an impressionable and breath taking one! You, yourself are a unique soul of your masterpiece.

So it is, and so mote it be!

About the Author

Kim Dhaliwal, born raised, and educated in the UK, she is a holistic and spiritual healer/teacher, for over 15years. She has an ethos of a spiritual and holistic approach to each soul she encounters, to become the very best version of themselves.

From a very young age she was surrounded by Angels and spirit, and not fully grasping it. A life changing premonition finally opened her eyes to what she was blessed with, and consequently her healing journey commenced with a transition onto a divine spiritual path.

She thrives on her passion to overcome challenges of any negative beliefs and thought patterns that cause disruption in daily life through stress, unworthiness unhappiness, and negativity. She finds it is a huge honour, when all those she meets leave in an empowered, uplifted way to embrace a more positive life.

She has a client base from all 'walks of life' national and international. Her clients describe her as a happy, friendly, empathetic, gifted and knowledgeable "Earth Angel" and above all how the genuineness, and warmth of her aura made them so relaxed and at peace in her presence.